Studio Visual Steps

Quick Introduction to the iPad and iPhone

*Get to know the most important and new options
on your iPad or iPhone with iOS 10 step by step*

Visual Steps™
www.visualsteps.com

This book has been written using the Visual Steps™ method.
Cover design by Studio Willemien Haagsma bNO

© 2016 Visual Steps
Author: Studio Visual Steps

First printing: November 2016
ISBN 978 90 5905 433 2

Resources used: A number of definitions and explanations of computer terminology are taken over from the *iPad User Guide* or the *iPhone User Guide*.

Do you have questions or suggestions?
E-mail: info@visualsteps.com

Would you like more information?
www.visualsteps.com

Website for this book:
www.visualsteps.com/quickios10

Subscribe to the free Visual Steps Newsletter:
www.visualsteps.com/newsletter

Table of Contents

Foreword

Dear readers,

Apple's latest operating system *iOS 10* will turn your iPhone or iPad into an even more convenient device with lots of new features. For example, you can receive notifications from your apps, messages and news in the renewed *Notification Center*. You can respond back right from there, if necessary.

Other good news is the enhanced *Messages* app. Have you ever sent a text message with balloons or confetti imagery? That is one of the new possibilities in *iOS 10*. You can also 'like' a message you have received as an SMS or *iMessage*. Or even send an applause if you agree with another person's SMS.

Apps are the heart of your iPhone or iPad. You can add and remove apps. New in *iOS 10* and after a lot of feedback, Apple is finally allowing you to delete the default apps that you never use. With *Safari*, you can surf the Internet, open as many tabs as you like and play in-line videos. You can also plan a route more conveniently in the much improved *Maps* app. Voice assistant *Siri* answers your spoken questions and will seek information for you.

Almost everyone takes a photo once in a while with his iPhone or iPad. The new *iOS 10* includes incredibly useful and fun ways to edit your photos. It is now possible to write on photos by hand, share them, magnify certain parts and add text blocks.

This book also deals with the topic music. You can transfer music from your PC to your iPad or iPhone, and listen to it whenever and wherever you want. You can try out the *Apple Music* service for three months. Listening to music via *streaming* is becoming ever more popular. You can decide for yourself whether this is something for you too; and in any case, the trial subscription will automatically stop if you follow our instructions.

Have fun exploring *iOS 10* for iPad and iPhone!

Saskia van Weert-Berghout
Studio Visual Steps

P.S. We welcome your comments and suggestions. Our email address is:
info@visualsteps.com

Introduction to Visual Steps™

The Visual Steps handbooks and manuals are the best instructional materials available for learning how to work with the iPad, iPhone, computers and other devices. Nowhere else can you find better support for getting to know an iPad or iPhone, the Internet, *Windows*, *MacOS*, a Samsung Galaxy Tab and computer programs.

Properties of the Visual Steps books:
- **Comprehensible contents**
  Addresses the needs of the beginner or intermediate computer user for a manual written in simple, straight-forward English.
- **Clear structure**
  Precise, easy to follow instructions. The material is broken down into small enough segments to allow for easy absorption.
- **Screen shots of every step**
  Quickly compare what you see on your screen with the screen shots in the book. Pointers and tips guide you when new windows are opened so you always know what to do next.
- **Get started right away**
  All you have to do is turn on your device and have your book at hand. Follow the steps as indicated on your own device.
- **Layout**
  The text is printed in a large size font and is clearly legible.

In short, I believe these manuals will be excellent guides for you.

dr. H. van der Meij
Faculty of Applied Education, Department of Instructional Technology, University of Twente, the Netherlands

What Do You Need?

To be able to work through this book, you will need a number of things:

 An iPad or iPhone with *iOS 10* or higher.

A computer or laptop with the *iTunes* program already installed. You can download *iTunes* yourself from the web page www.apple.com/itunes/download.

If you do not own a computer or laptop, you may be able to perform certain necessary actions, such as transferring photos, using a computer from a friend or family member. A computer is however not necessary for working with an iPad or iPhone. You can just read the instructions instead.

Tip
Glossary at the end of the book
Appendix A. Glossary provides a summary and description of frequently used terms in this book.

How to Use This Book

This book has been written using the Visual Steps™ method. The method is simple: you place the book next to your iPad or iPhone and execute all the tasks step by step, directly on your device. With the clear instructions and the multitude of screen shots, you will always know exactly what to do. This is the quickest way to become familiar with the iPad or iPhone with *iOS 10*.

In this Visual Steps™ book, you will see various icons. This is what they mean:

Techniques
These icons indicate an action to be carried out:

	The index finger indicates you need to do something on the iPad's or iPhone's screen, for instance, tap something, or type a text.

	The keyboard icon means you should type something on the keyboard of your iPad, iPhone or your computer.

	The mouse icon means you should do something on your computer with the mouse.

	The hand icon means you should do something else, for example rotate the iPad or iPhone or switch it off. The hand is also used for a series of operations which you have learned at an earlier stage.

Apart from these operations, in some parts of this book extra assistance is provided to help you successfully work through this book.

Help
These icons indicate that extra help is available:

 The arrow icon warns you about something.

 The bandage icon will help you if something has gone wrong.

 Have you forgotten how to do something? The number next to the footsteps tells you where to look it up at the end of the book in the appendix *How Do I Do That Again?*

In separate boxes you will find general information or tips concerning the iPad.

Extra information
Information boxes are denoted by these icons:

 The book icon gives you extra background information that you can read at your convenience. This extra information is not necessary for working through the book.

 The light bulb icon indicates an extra tip for using the device, program or service.

Visual Steps Newsletter

All Visual Steps books follow the same methodology: clear and concise step-by-step instructions with screen shots to demonstrate each task. A complete list of all our books can be found on our website **www.visualsteps.com** You can also sign up to receive our **free Visual Steps Newsletter**.
In this Newsletter you will receive periodic information by email regarding:
- the latest titles and previously released books;
- special offers, supplemental chapters, tips and free informative booklets.
Also, our Newsletter subscribers may download any of the documents listed on the web pages **www.visualsteps.com/info_downloads**
When you subscribe to our Newsletter you can be assured that we will never use your email address for any purpose other than sending you the information as previously described. We will not share this address with any third-party. Each Newsletter also contains a one-click link to unsubscribe.

Website

On the website that accompanies this book, **www.visualsteps.com/quickios10**, you will find more information about this book. This website will also keep you informed of changes you need to know as a user of the book. Visit this website regularly and check if there are any recent updates or additions to this book, or possible errata.

Test Your Knowledge

After you have worked through this book, you can test your knowledge online, at the **www.ccforseniors.com** website.

By answering a number of multiple choice questions you will be able to test your knowledge. After you have finished a test, you will receive a *Computer Certificate*. Participating in the test is **free of charge**. The computer certificate website is a free Visual Steps service.

For Teachers

The Visual Steps books have been written as self-study guides for individual use. Although these books also well suited for use in a group or a classroom setting. For this purpose, some of our books come with a free teacher's manual. You can download the available teacher's manuals and additional materials at: **www.visualsteps.com/instructor**
After you have registered at this website, you can use this service for free.

The Screen Shots

The screen shots in this book indicate which button, file or hyperlink you need to tap on your iPad or iPhone screen or click on your computer. In the instruction text (in **bold** letters) you will see a small image of the item you need to tap or click. The line will point you to the right place on your screen.
The small screen shots that are printed in this book are not meant to be completely legible all the time. This is not necessary, as you will see these images on your own iPad or iPhone screen in real size and fully legible.

On the next page you see an example of an instruction text and a screen shot of the item you need to click. The line indicates where to find this item on your own screen.

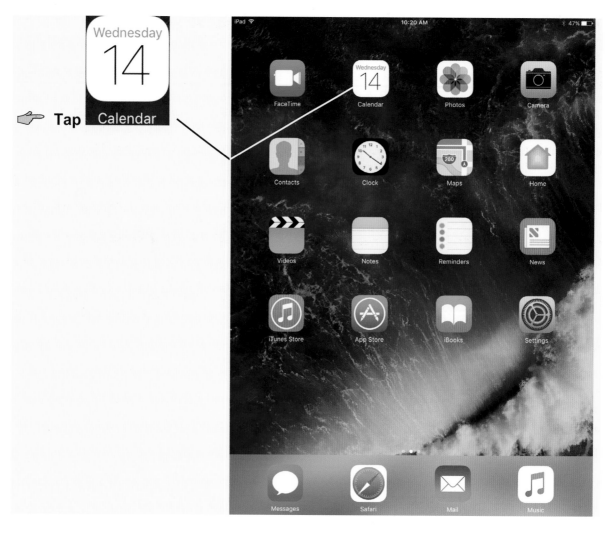

☞ **Tap** Calendar

In some cases, the screen shot only displays part of the screen. Below you see an example of this:

At the bottom of the screen:

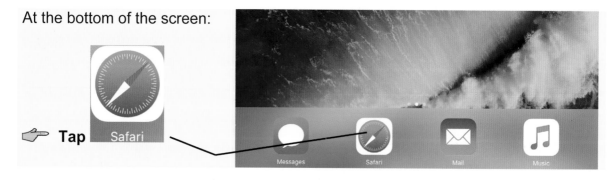

☞ **Tap** Safari

We would like to emphasize that we **do not intend you** to read the information in all of the screen shots in this book. Always use the screen shots in combination with the display on your own device.

1. Using the iPad and iPhone

iOS 10 is Apple's latest operating system for the iPad and iPhone. At first glance, things may look very similar to the previous *iOS 9* version. But you will soon encounter a variety of options and accessories that can make working with your device a lot faster, more convenient and comfortable.

Once you have installed the update, you will notice this right away. Unlocking the iPad or iPhone is done in a different way as the 'Slide to Unlock' feature has been eliminated and Touch ID now plays a bigger role. You will also see a new Home app on your screen.

Changes to the *Notification Center* allow greater interaction with apps and 3D Touch sensitivity. A new *Widgets* panel can also be activated by swiping to the right.

In this chapter you learn how to:

- unlock your device;
- install a new background;
- search through the settings;
- turn off motion;
- look for updates;
- set up and use Touch ID and a passcode;
- work with the *Notification Center* and the *Control Center;*
- turn on the *Do Not Disturb* feature.

 Please note:

If you purchased this book, you either want to change from an earlier version of *iOS* to *iOS 10* for iPad or iPhone, or you have worked with a tablet or smartphone with an *Android* operating system. In any case, working with a tablet or smartphone is not completely unknown to you. You will soon see that some of the instructions and actions described in this book you are already familiar with, but others not. This book focuses primarily on the new features in *iOS 10* for the iPad or iPhone.

 Please note:

Most of the screenshots in this book were made on an iPad. If you have an iPhone, the screens may look slightly different. If there are any differences in the steps needed to carry out a certain action, they will be noted.

1.1 Unlocking the iPad and iPhone

In *iOS 10* you unlock the iPad or iPhone in a different way than in the previous versions of *iOS*. This is how you unlock your device:

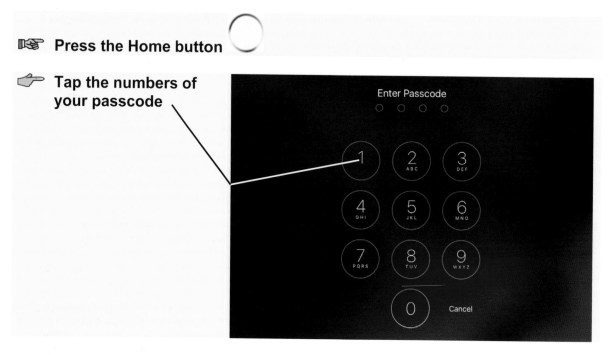

☞ **Press the Home button**

☞ **Tap the numbers of your passcode**

Have you set up Touch ID?

☞ **Place your fingertip on**

The device unlocks and you see the home screen with its standard apps and possibly a few apps that you have downloaded yourself.
You may also notice a different background. This background can be seen on new devices being used for the first time. If you have upgraded to *iOS 10* on a device you have already been using, you will see the previous background that had been configured. If you do not like the background, you can select a new one:

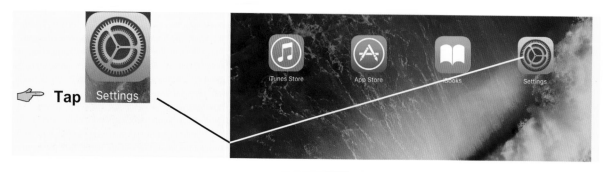

☞ **Tap** Settings

👉 **Tap** Wallpaper

👉 **Tap**
Choose a New Wallp

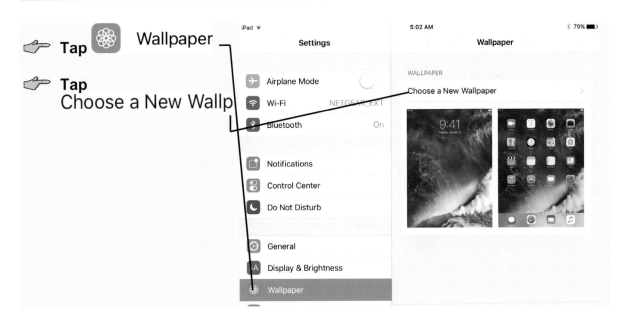

The option to use dynamic backgrounds was already present in the previous version, but you may want to take another look at it now. To set up a dynamic background:

👉 **Tap** Dynamic

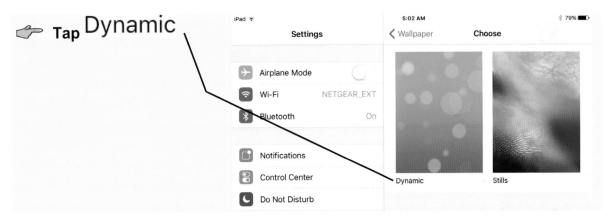

There are dynamic backgrounds available in various colors:

👉 **Tap a background**

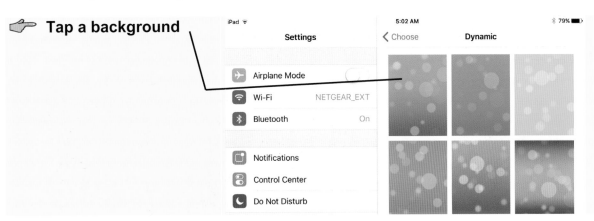

You see a preview of the new animated background. To set this for both the lock and the home screen:

☞ **Tap** Set Both ⟍

If you prefer, you can select the new background for just one of the options, either the **Set Lock Screen** or the **Set Home Screen**.

☞ **Press the Home button**

Moving circles will appear:

Notice how the circles react when you move your iPad or iPhone:

☞ **Tilt the iPad or iPhone towards you or to the left or right**

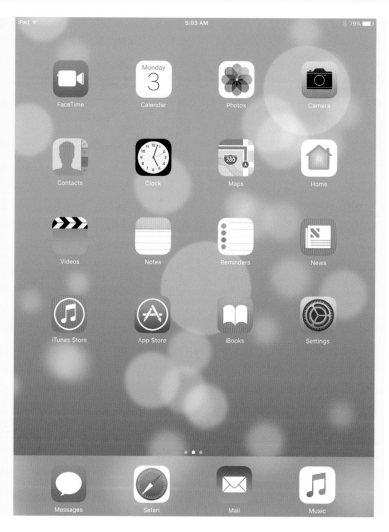

If the moving circles are too much of a distraction, you can set the background to a more static type:

☞ **Tap** Settings , ‹ Choose, Stills

You see a number of backgrounds. You can view more backgrounds as follows:

☞ **Drag upwards over the backgrounds**

☞ **Tap the desired background**

In this book the standard background will be used.

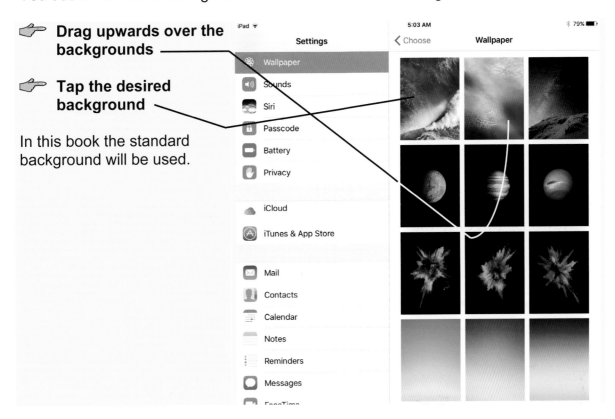

In this example the standard background has been selected again for both the lock and the home screen:

☞ **Tap** Set Both

☞ **Tap** ‹ Choose, ‹ Wallpaper

☞ **Press the Home button**

1.2 Searching in Settings

In the *Settings* app, you can search for the items you want to set up or change on your iPad and iPhone:

☞ **Tap** Settings

You can search for an option or feature that you do not see directly. You can use *Settings* for example, to disable the keyboard sound:

☞ **If necessary, scroll the menu on the left side of the screen downwards**

You now see the search field at the top of the screen:

If for example, you want to enable or disable the keyboard sound, you can proceed as follows:

☞ **Tap the search field**

⌨ **Type:** Key

You will see results while you type:

☞ **Tap**

🔊 Keyboard Clicks
Sounds

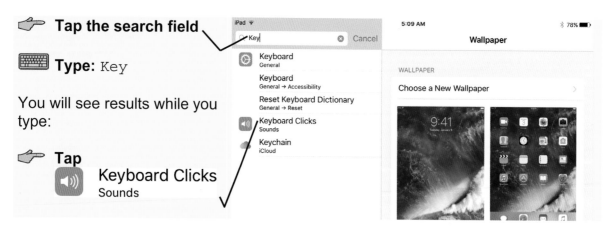

The *Sounds* app appears. The slider control to switch the keyboard clicks to on or off, is not directly visible. First you need to hide the keyboard. On the keyboard:

☞ **Tap**

Now you see the slider control to switch the keyboard clicks on or off:

By default, the keyboard clicks option is set to on. To switch it to off:

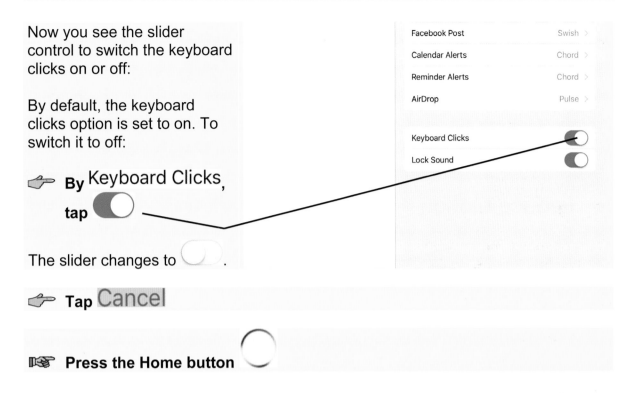

☞ **By** Keyboard Clicks,

tap

The slider changes to .

☞ **Tap** Cancel

☞ **Press the Home button**

1.3 Reducing Motion

Are your apps sorted in folders? *iOS 10* includes new animations or movements that will play as soon as you open an app. This is also called the parallax effect. Disabling these animations ensures a longer lasting battery.

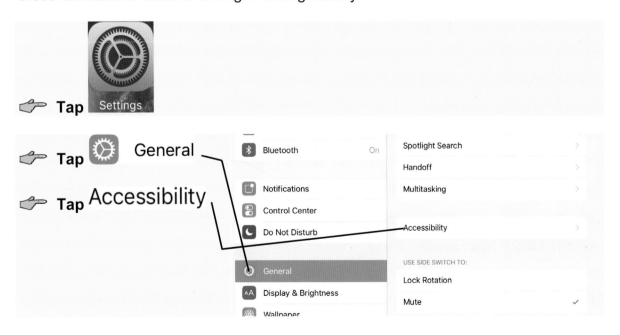

☞ **Tap** Settings

☞ **Tap** General

☞ **Tap** Accessibility

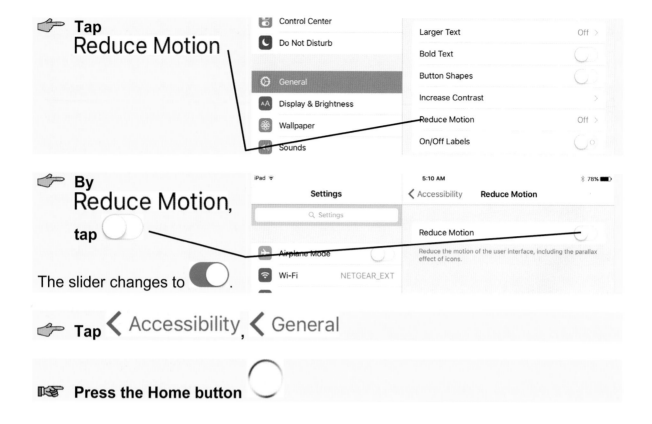

Tap
Reduce Motion

By
Reduce Motion,

tap

The slider changes to .

Tap ‹ Accessibility, ‹ General

☞ **Press the Home button**

1.4 Searching for Updates

Apple releases updates for the iPad and iPhone on a regular basis. In time, these will be brought to your attention by a message on your screen. It may take a while for you to receive such a message. But you can also check for yourself if a new update is available, for example, after you heard about it or read something in the news.

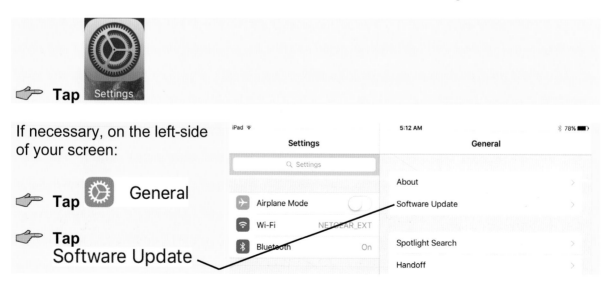

☞ **Tap** Settings

If necessary, on the left-side of your screen:

☞ **Tap** General

☞ **Tap** Software Update

In most cases you see Your software is up to date. If, however an update is available, you will see information about the update and can follow the on-screen instructions to download and install it.

 Tip

Installing iOS updates at night

If a new update is available for your iPad or iPhone, you can choose to install it at night. When you start the installation, you can choose 'Install later'. The update will then be installed overnight between 02:00 and 05:00 AM.

1.5 Touch ID

Most new models of iPads and iPhones are equipped with Touch ID. On the device, the Home button contains a fingerprint scanner that allows you to do different things. First, you can quickly unlock your device with your finger without the required passcode. Also, you can quickly log on to apps that are suitable for that purpose. Touch ID can be set during the installation of a new iPhone or iPad. But it can also be set up later in the *Settings* app. In this section, this is demonstrated on an iPhone. The procedure is very similar on an iPad.

☞ **Tap** Settings

☞ **If necessary, drag the menu upwards**

☞ **Tap** Touch ID & Passcode

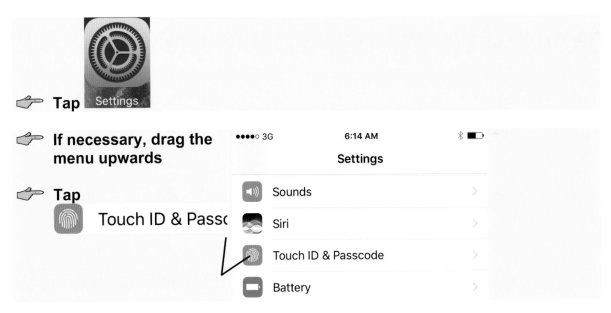

 Please note:

If you only see the 🔒 Passcode option in *Settings*, this means the Touch ID feature is not available on your device. Only the newer models of the iPhone and iPad are equipped with a fingerprint scanner and Touch ID.

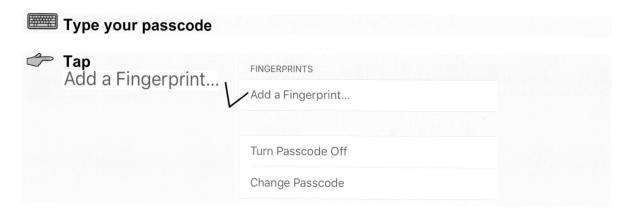

Type your passcode

Tap
Add a Fingerprint...

Now you see some information on adding a fingerprint. You can proceed:

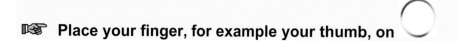

Place your finger, for example your thumb, on

iOS scans your finger. The idea is that you lift your finger briefly and rotate a little when the device vibrates. The red lines in the signed fingerprint indicate how much of your fingerprint is scanned already. Unfortunately, we cannot show any pictures of this process. Tap OK, as soon as you see instructions on placing your finger.

Tap Continue

iOS will proceed with the scanning. Again, you have to lift and rotate your finger briefly when the device vibrates.

Tap Continue

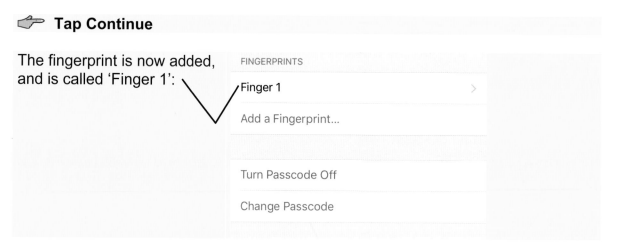

The fingerprint is now added, and is called 'Finger 1':

The fingerprint is now ready to use. In the future you can unlock your iPhone or iPad after you press the Home button.

Would you like to add another fingerprint, from your other hand for example?

☞ **Tap**
Add a Fingerprint...

Follow the instructions again, but touch the scanner with another finger than you did just now. Many people scan both thumbs and index fingers. This way, in most cases, you can unlock the phone or tablet with the hand that carries the device.

☞ **Follow the instructions on the screen**

When you are finished:

☞ **Press the Home button** 〇

1.6 Passcode

You can also add a passcode for unlocking the device. This code can contain six numbers.

☞ **Tap** Settings

In the top right of the screen on the iPad or after scrolling the menu downwards on iPhone:

☞ **Tap** 🔒 Passcode *or* 👆 Touch ID & Passcode

⌨ **Type your current passcode**

If you want to change your current code:

☞ **Tap**
Change Passcode

⌨ **Type your current passcode**

If you have not yet used a passcode:

☞ **Tap** Turn Passcode On

You can choose a six-numbered code:

☞ **Tap**
Passcode Options

☞ **Tap**
6-Digit Numeric Code

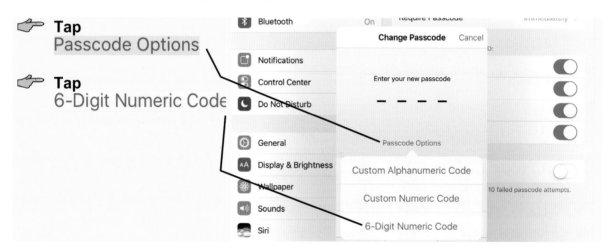

You can enter the new passcode:

☞ **Tap the desired six**
numbers for the
passcode

In the next screen:

 Tap again the same six numbers for the passcode

 Press the Home button

Your iPad or iPhone is now secured with a passcode of six numbers.

If you find it inconvenient to have to type a password each time you unlock the iPad or iPhone, you can remove the code as follows:

 Tap Settings

Tap Passcode

Type your current passcode

Tap Turn Passcode Off

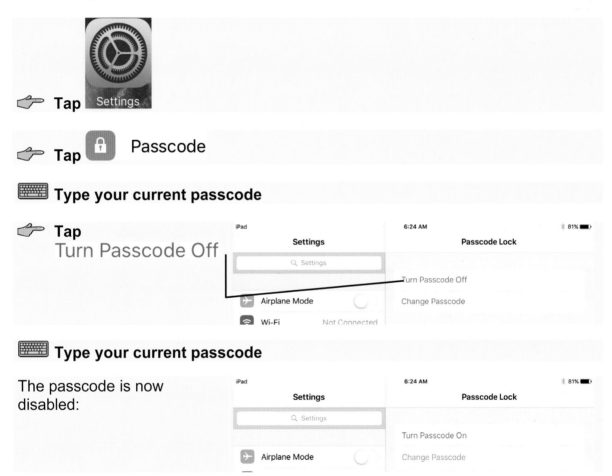

Type your current passcode

The passcode is now disabled:

Now you are no longer prompted for a password when you turn on the iPad or iPhone. Also, Touch ID is turned off. However, the fingerprints will be retained. If you want to reactivate a passcode in the future, you will be asked to keep or delete the stored fingerprints. If you keep them, you will not need to scan your fingers again.

 **Press the Home button**

Please note:

An iPad or iPhone without passcode may sound convenient as it lets you skip some typing or other gestures. But if your device is stolen or falls into the wrong hands, it could prove very risky. Without the additional security, someone might be able to use your apps, read your email or even send out one in your name, if your email is already set up. It is therefore advisable to use a passcode.

 Tip

Adjusting the screen's stand-by time

By default, the screen of the iPad or iPhone will turn off after two minutes of inactivity. If you want to set a longer or shorter time, you can adjust this setting as follows:

👉 **Tap** Settings , AA Display & Brightness , Auto-Lock

👉 **Tap the desired time**

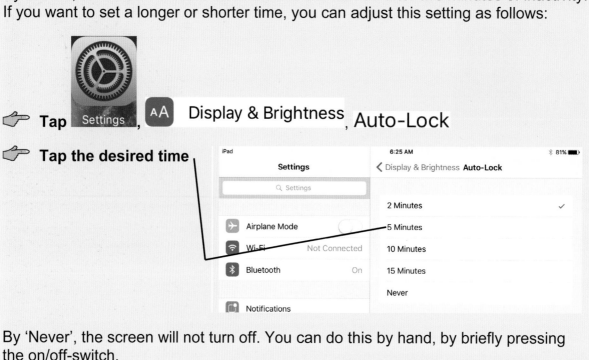

By 'Never', the screen will not turn off. You can do this by hand, by briefly pressing the on/off-switch.

👉 **Tap** ‹ Display & Brightness

☞ **Press the Home button** ⬭

1.7 Notification Center

Notification Center is the central location where you can see a list of notifications or alerts from a number of apps. For example, if there is an appointment in your calendar for today or a new email or text message, you will find it there.

To open the *Notification Center:*

 Swipe down from the top of the screen

The *Notification Center* consists of two pages. The first page contains widgets, the second page contains notifications from your apps. If you have not used any apps, this page will be empty and will display the message No Notifications. You can just continue reading.

You see notifications from various apps. They are sorted by date: ———

To open a notification:

 Tap the notification

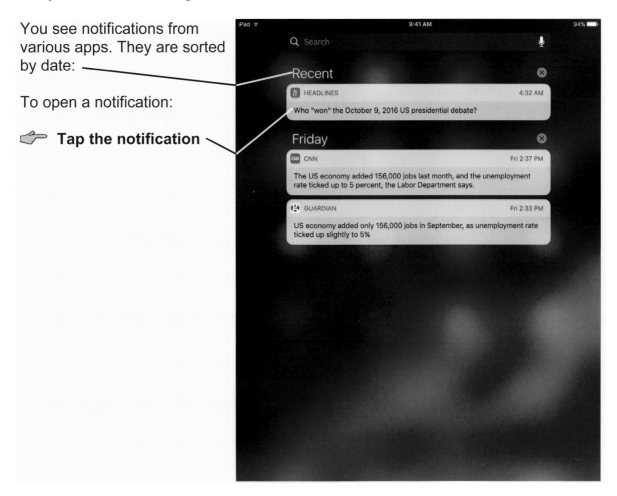

The app related to the notification will open. You can read for example a news flash, if that is what you tapped. To open the *Notification Center* again:

 Swipe down from the top of the screen

You may see a different background relating to the contours of the app you just opened. Once you have read a notification it is no longer displayed in the list.

Not all notifications are urgent or even interesting and you may want to delete some of them right away. New in *iOS 10* is that notifications shown for the same day in *Notification Center* can be deleted all at once.

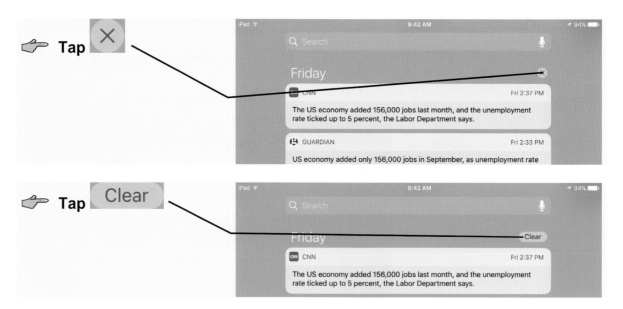

☞ **Tap** ×

☞ **Tap** Clear

Repeat this for every day you want to delete its notifications. Once everything is deleted, you will see No Notifications.

Now you can take a look at the widgets section:

☞ **Swipe the screen from the left to the right**

You see the widgets section of the *Notification Center*:

If you gave permission for it, you will see the weather forecast at the top:

Underneath, notifications from your calendar are displayed:

If you tap the notification, it opens in the calendar. You do not need to do this now.

You can learn more about widgets in *Chapter 3 Apps*.

You can close the *Notification Center*:

☞ **Swipe up from the bottom of the screen**

In the *Settings* app you can select per app which notifications should be displayed in the *Notification Center*. By default, email messages are not displayed in the *Notification Center*. But you can allow them to be displayed if you want:

☞ **Tap** Settings, **Notifications**

You see what kind of notifications are shown per app:

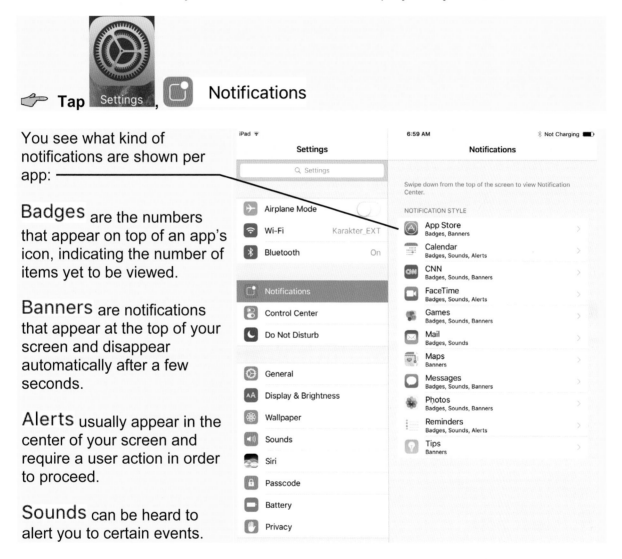

Badges are the numbers that appear on top of an app's icon, indicating the number of items yet to be viewed.

Banners are notifications that appear at the top of your screen and disappear automatically after a few seconds.

Alerts usually appear in the center of your screen and require a user action in order to proceed.

Sounds can be heard to alert you to certain events.

In this screen you cannot see which apps are displayed in the *Notification Center*. To find out, you need to take a look at the settings for each individual app.

If you want to display notifications for new email, you will need to have an email account already set up:

☞ **Tap**   **Mail**   Badges, Sounds

☞ **If necessary, tap the desired email account**

If you have only one email account set up, you will see this screen right away.

To display new email notifications in the *Notification Center*:

☞ **By** Show in Notification Center **tap**

The slider changes to 🔘.

New email will now be displayed in the *Notification Center*.

By default, notifications are not shown for new email:

But if desired, you can allow an alert to be displayed every time you receive a new email. You can also set the style for the alert:

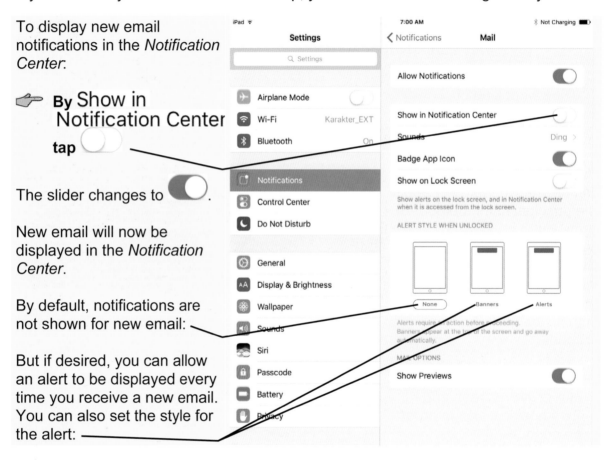

🖐 **Please note:**
The *Notification Center* can also be accessed from the lock screen, before you enter the access code. To prevent other people from viewing the notifications for a specific app, you can keep the option to Show on Lock Screen off.

☞ **Press the Home button**

1.8 Control Center

The *Control Center* has multiple panels that give you quick access to a number of settings, controls and basic functions on the iPad or iPhone:

☞ **Swipe up from the bottom of the screen**

If you are using the *Control Center* for the first time, an introduction window appears:

☞ **Tap Continue**

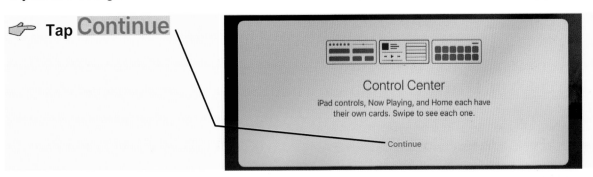

You see an assortment of icons in the *Control Center*. The principal ones are:

✈ Tap to turn on airplane mode to disable the Internet and phone connection:

📶 Tap to enable or disable Wi-Fi:

✻ Tap to enable and disable Bluetooth:

🌙 Tap to switch the *Do Not Disturb* option on or off:

Night Shift: Off Tap to control the brightness of the screen when it is getting dark:

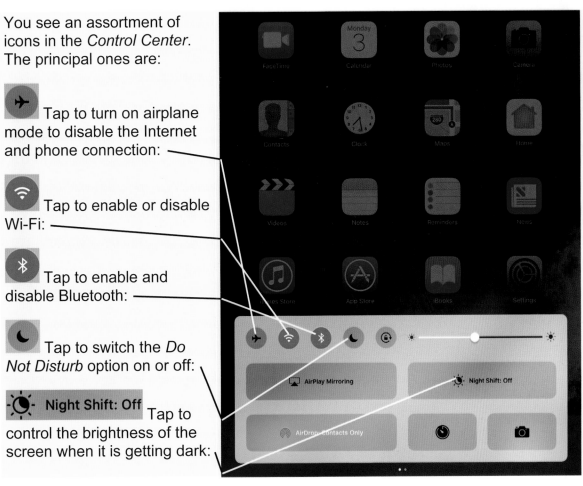

New in the *Control Center* in *iOS 10* is a separate pane called *Now Playing*. Take a look at this now:

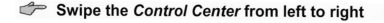 **Swipe the *Control Center* from right to left**

You see the new pane, featuring music and playback controls. You can read more about playing music in *iOS 10* in *Chapter 5 Music and Apple Music*. To go back to the first page:

☞ **Swipe the *Control Center* from left to right**

1.9 Do Not Disturb

When you use the iPad or iPhone for contacting others, you will probably receive messages on a regular basis. For example, someone has sent you a message or you tried to call someone with the *FaceTime* app. These messages appear on your iPad or iPhone and if the sound is on, you will hear a tone. But there are times when you do not want to be disturbed by these sounds. For this you can use the *Do Not Disturb* feature. You can activate this in the *Control Center* as follows:

☞ **If necessary, swipe up from the bottom of the screen**

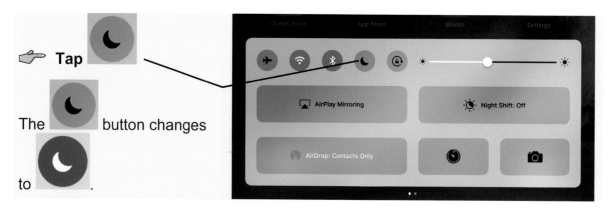

☞ **Tap**

The   button changes

to   .

☞ **Swipe down over the *Control Center***

You will not receive any notifications until you tap the  button again in the *Control Center* to disable it. Keep in mind that if you use *FaceTime*, incoming *FaceTime* calls will also be blocked. It is also possible to automatically block messages for a fixed period of time, for example, while you sleep. To do that:

☞ **Tap** Settings

The moon symbol in the status bar indicates that the *Do Not Disturb* function is turned on:

☞ **Tap** Do Not Disturb

☞ **By** Scheduled, **tap**

The slider changes to .

The moon disappears from the status bar. There are a number of adjustable settings:

By default, the notifications and incoming *FaceTime* calls between 10:00PM and 07:00AM are blocked. You can change the times here:

Optionally, you can specify the contacts whose *FaceTime* calls will not be blocked:

The option Repeated Calls ensures that someone who makes a second *FaceTime* call within three minutes is not blocked:

By default, *FaceTime* calls and notifications are allowed as long as the device is unlocked:

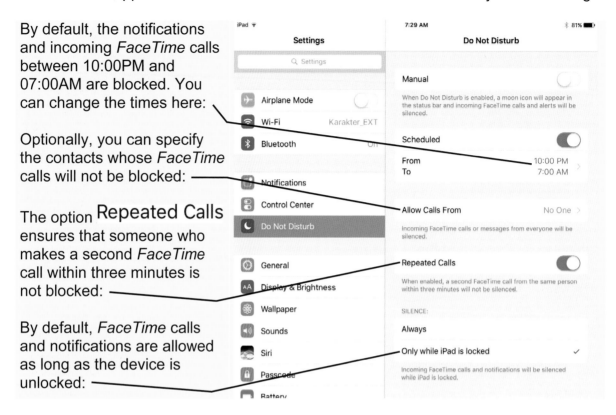

By setting the notifications on your iPad or iPhone to suit your needs and using the *Do Not Disturb* option and other apps wisely, you will be disturbed much less often.

☞ **Press the Home button**

In this chapter you have learned to work with some options on the iPad and iPhone. I'm sure you will often use these options in the future.

1.10 Tips

 Tip

Raise to wake

iOS 10 contains a new feature called *Raise to Wake*. This feature is only available on the iPhone 6S, 6SE, 7 and newer. When you lift the device, the screen turns on automatically without having to unlock the iPhone. This lets you get a quick glance at notifications such as incoming email or text messages.

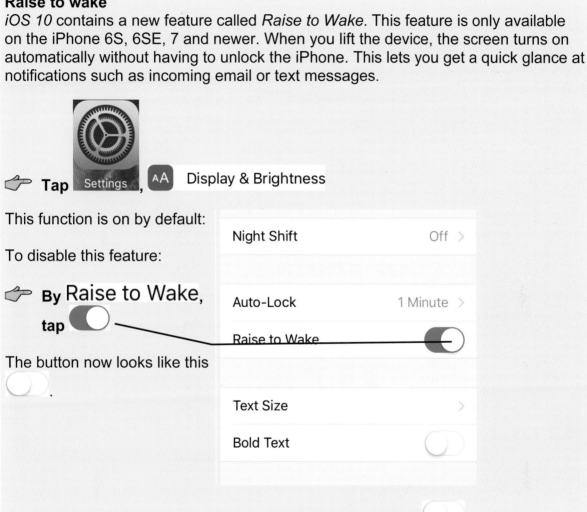

☞ **Tap** Settings , AA Display & Brightness

This function is on by default:

To disable this feature:

☞ **By Raise to Wake, tap** ⬤

Night Shift	Off >
Auto-Lock	1 Minute >
Raise to Wake	⬤
Text Size	>
Bold Text	◯

The button now looks like this ◯ .

To turn this feature on again, repeat the same steps and tap ◯ .

Tip

Turning off all notifications

If you do not want to see a certain app's notifications anymore, you can turn them off as follows:

 By

Allow Notification

tap

The slider changes to ⬭ .

 Tip

Turning off Bluetooth

In every upgrade, Apple turns on Bluetooth on your iPad or iPhone. If you do not use any Bluetooth devices, it is better to turn this feature off and save your battery.

☞ **Swipe up from the bottom of the screen**

☞ **Tap**

The 🔵 button changes to

⬛ .

Bluetooth is now disabled. To turn Bluetooth on again, repeat the same steps and

tap the 🔵 button once more.

2. Mail, SMS and Messages

Your iPhone and iPad are equipped with an email app called *Mail*. *Mail* lets you write, send and receive email. In this chapter you can learn how to set up your email account for email addresses from Outlook.com. These include email addresses ending with outlook.com or hotmail.com. We also describe how to send, receive and delete an email.

With the *Messages* app you can send messages (SMS or *iMessages*) to other people. This app contains many new features such as balloons and effects, and you also have the ability to draw with your fingers on the screen.

You can still use the iPhone to call people, of course, and you can add new contacts to your phone. Notifications about calls arrive in the *Notification Center*. New in *iOS 10* is that you can call back directly from that same screen.

In this chapter you learn how to:

- set up an email account;
- send, receive and delete emails;
- add contacts;
- send messages (SMS or *iMessages*);
- use message bubble animations;
- view notifications in the *Notification Center*;
- delete notifications;
- answer messages straight from the *Notification Center*;
- call with the iPhone.

2.1 Set Up an Email Account

Before you can email with the *Mail* app, you must have an email account set up on your iPad or iPhone. This section explains how to do that for an Outlook.com account; an email address ending with outlook.com or hotmail.com. You can set a *Gmail* email address in a similar manner. You will need your email address and related password.

 HELP! I have another email address.

If you want to use another email address, for example, from your Internet provider, you can read the *Tip* at the end of this chapter and learn how to set it up in *Mail*.

☞ **Tap** Settings

☞ **If necessary, scroll the menu on the left side of the screen upwards**

☞ **Tap** ✉ Mail

☞ **Tap** Accounts

☞ **Tap** Add Account

☞ **Tap** Outlook.com

In this example an email address ending with hotmail.com is used. You can follow the same steps for an email address ending with outlook.com. To set the email address, you need to have your login information ready:

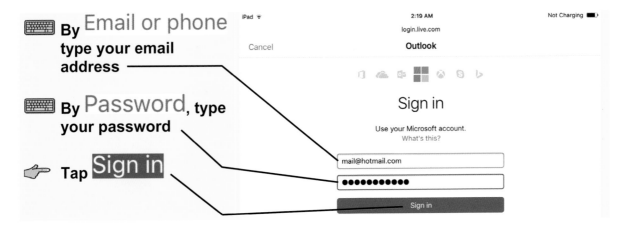

Now you need your iPad or iPhone to get access to your account. This is necessary for receiving email and, for example, for using data from your online calendar in the *Calendar* app.

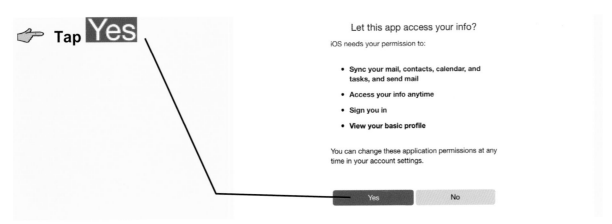

The iPad or iPhone recognize the server automatically. In the next screen, select whether you want to sync contacts and calendars as well as email. In this example, these settings are not changed:

☞ **Tap** ❮ Mail

☞ **Press the Home button** ⭕

2.2 Sending an Email

For sending and receiving email, you can use the *Mail* app:

At the bottom of the screen:

☞ **Tap** [Mail]

☞ **If necessary, tap** ❮ Inbox **and then** ❮ Mailboxes

The device will check for new messages. In this example, there are no new messages, but on your device there possibly are. You can open a new, blank email:

☞ **Tap** [✎]

On your iPhone you will see this icon at the bottom right of your screen:

A new message is opened. You can practice sending a test email to yourself:

⌨ **By** To:**, type your email address**

⚲ **Tip**

Contacts

When you tap the ⊕ icon, you open the contact list. You can select the recipient from the list by tapping his or her name. Or you can just start typing the first letter of a contact name whose email address you saved. Immediately you will see a selection from the contact list. The same happens when you type the first letter of a stored email address. Later on in this chapter you will learn how to add names to the contact list.

⌨ **By** Subject: **, type** Test

☞ **Tap the white area**

⌨ **Type:** This is a test.

You can continue on a new line:

☞ **Tap** return

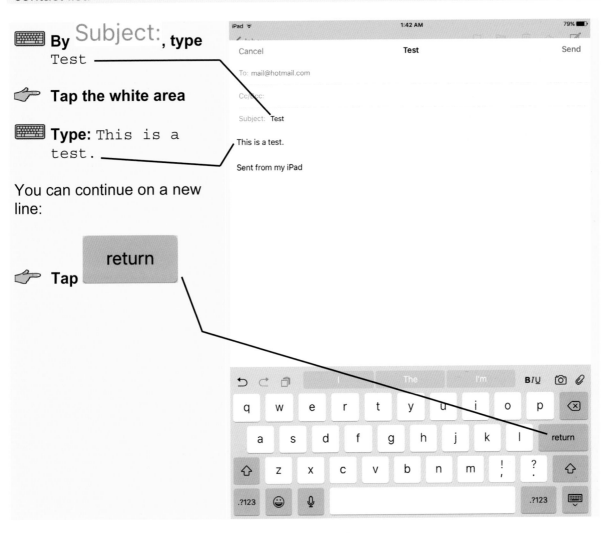

The iPad and iPhone are provided with a dictionary that helps you while you are typing, for example, if you type a spelling error:

Type: `Type a spelling eror`

As you type you see a suggested correction for the misspelled word:

error   :

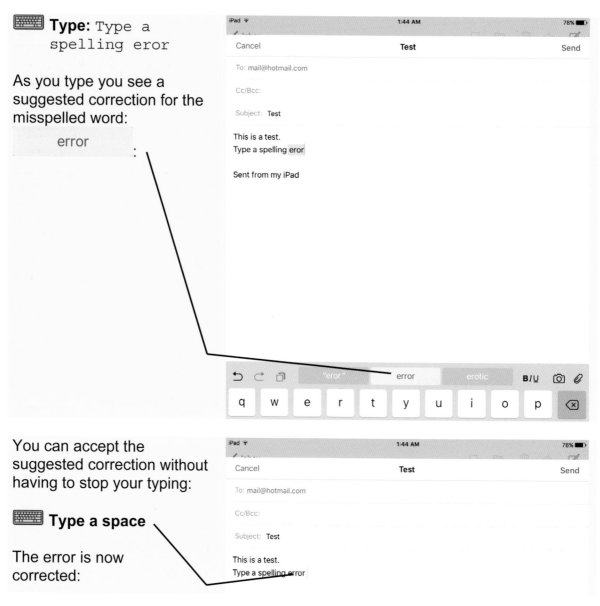

You can accept the suggested correction without having to stop your typing:

Type a space

The error is now corrected:

Tip

Corrections

A suggested adjustment is also accepted as you type a period, comma or other punctuation mark. You can also reject a proposed correction. You must do this before you type a space, period, comma or other punctuation mark, otherwise the correction is accepted.

☞ **Tap the corrected word**   error

If you are not satisfied with your typing, you can easily delete the text with the Backspace button:

☞ **Press your finger on**

until two lines are deleted ⟶

First, the deleting happens letter by letter. Once you reach the next line, the words are deleted one by one.

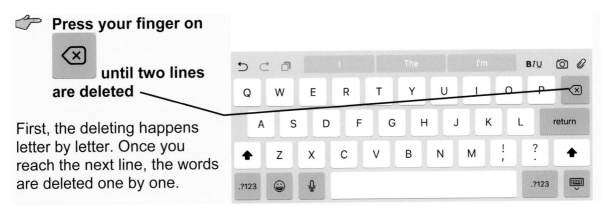

In the *Mail* app you can also copy, cut and paste text. You can do this word by word, or the entire text all at once. To select a word:

☞ **Place your finger on the word iPad** ⟶

A magnifying glass appears:

☞ **Release your finger**

A pop-up menu appears. You can choose to select a word, multiple words or the entire text. Select the word:

☞ **Tap** Select ⟶

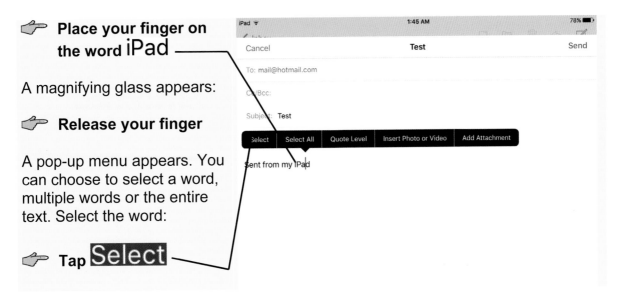

💡 **Tip**

Magnifying glass
If you place your finger on a word, a magnifying glass appears. With the magnifying glass, you can easily move the cursor to a specific place within a word or between words, for example, in order to change or correct the text.

The word is selected. To select more words, drag the sliders ┃ ╻. Now you can cut, copy or replace a word by a similar word (synonym). You can copy the word:

Tap Copy

The word is copied to the clipboard. You can paste it into the text:

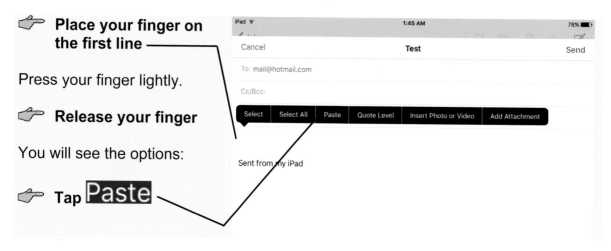

Place your finger on the first line

Press your finger lightly.

Release your finger

You will see the options:

Tap Paste

 Tip
Other apps
The actions that you have learned here, can be applied to other apps as well.

The copied word is now on the first line:

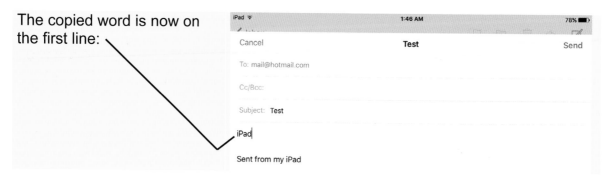

The text in the email message can also be formatted:

👉 **Select the word 'iPad' on the first line**

👉 **Tap** BIU

On the iPhone you first may need to tap ▶ to see BIU.

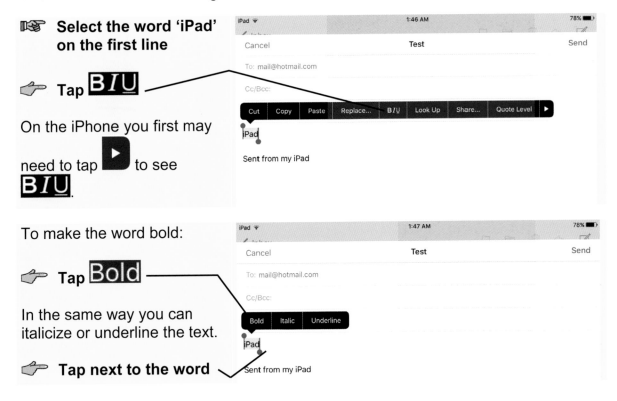

To make the word bold:

👉 **Tap** Bold

In the same way you can italicize or underline the text.

👉 **Tap next to the word**

Now you can send your test email:

👉 **Tap Send**

Your email is sent, and if the sound is on, you will hear a swishing sound or other tone.

2.3 Receiving an Email

Your message will be received automatically by *Mail*. Depending on the settings you have made, you may also hear a beep or other tone. You can open the *Inbox*, which holds your received messages:

👉 **If necessary, tap** ✉ Inbox

You can recognize an unread message by its blue dot :

☞ **Tap the received message**

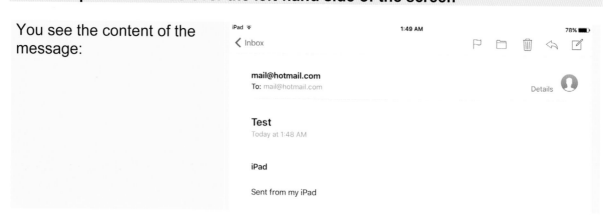 **HELP! Ik do not see a new message.**

If you do not see a new email message:

☞ **Swipe downwards over the left-hand side of the screen**

You see the content of the message:

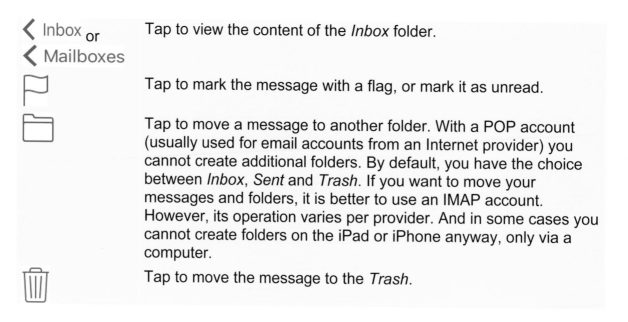

In the toolbars above or below the message you can see a number of icons. Here is what they do:

❮ Inbox or
❮ Mailboxes   Tap to view the content of the *Inbox* folder.

⚑   Tap to mark the message with a flag, or mark it as unread.

🗀   Tap to move a message to another folder. With a POP account (usually used for email accounts from an Internet provider) you cannot create additional folders. By default, you have the choice between *Inbox*, *Sent* and *Trash*. If you want to move your messages and folders, it is better to use an IMAP account. However, its operation varies per provider. And in some cases you cannot create folders on the iPad or iPhone anyway, only via a computer.

🗑   Tap to move the message to the *Trash*.

Tap to reply, forward or print message.

Tap to compose a new message.

2.4 Deleting an Email

You can delete the test message:

 Tap 🗑

On your iPhone you see this icon at the bottom of the screen.

The email is moved to the *Trash*.

👉 Please note:

In some types of email accounts, such as *Gmail*, a deleted email is first moved to the *Trash*, but is not deleted right away.

You can now verify this:

👉 **Tap** ❮ Inbox **or** ❮ Mailboxes

👉 **Tap** ❮ Mailboxes

👉 **If necessary, tap the desired email account**

You see a number of folders:

👉 **Tap** 🗑 Trash

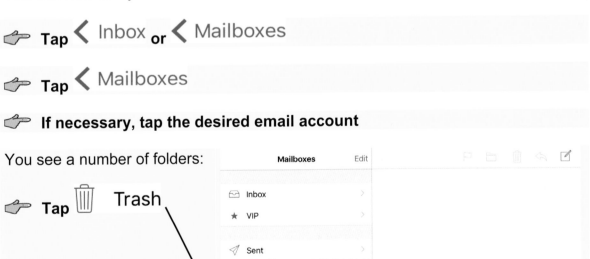

You will find the deleted message in the *Trash.* You can delete the message permanently as follows:

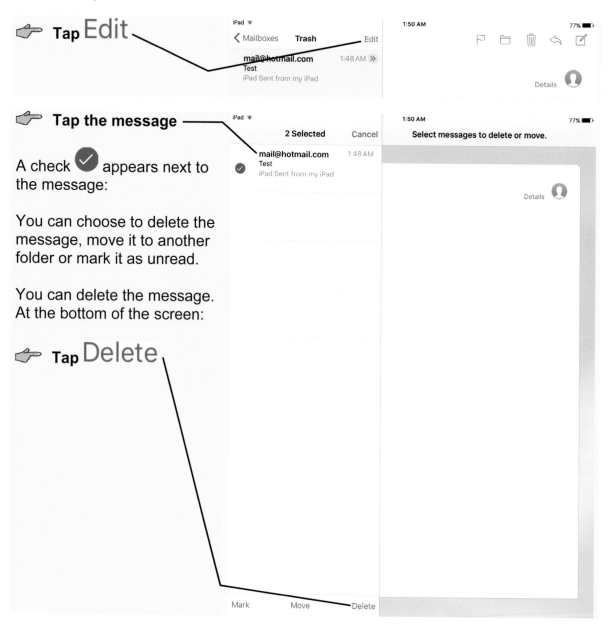

☞ **Tap** Edit

☞ **Tap the message**

A check ✓ appears next to the message:

You can choose to delete the message, move it to another folder or mark it as unread.

You can delete the message. At the bottom of the screen:

☞ **Tap** Delete

💡 **Tip**

Deleting all messages
If you want to delete all messages at once, you do not have to tap each individual message, instead:

☞ **Tap** Delete All, Delete All

To return to the *Inbox*:

☞ **If necessary, tap the name of your account**

☞ **Tap** ❮ Mailboxes

📭 **Press the Home button** ⭕

2.5 Adding Contacts

You can add new contacts in the *Contacts* app. The advantage is that you can call someone in the future by viewing the name instead of the phone number:

☞ **Tap** Contacts

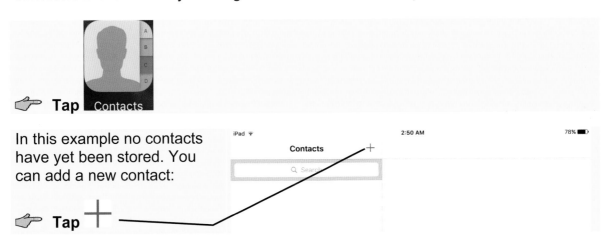

In this example no contacts have yet been stored. You can add a new contact:

☞ **Tap** ╋

Here, a fictional contact is added as an example, but if you want, you can enter the details of a person you know. You do this using the onscreen keyboard:

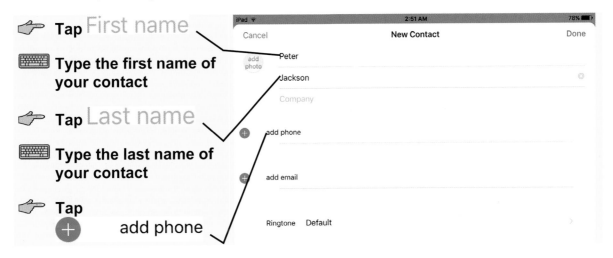

☞ **Tap** First name

⌨ **Type the first name of your contact**

☞ **Tap** Last name

⌨ **Type the last name of your contact**

☞ **Tap** ⊕ add phone

Type the mobile number of your contact

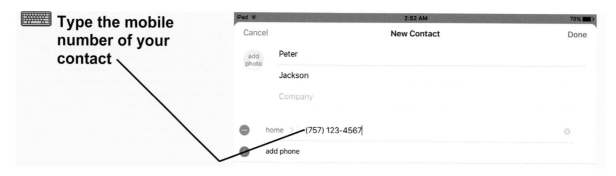

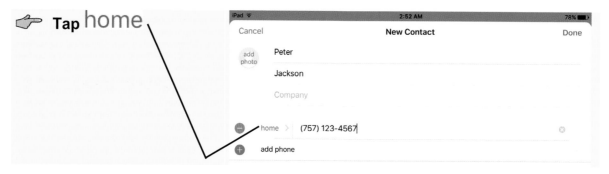

🦅 **Please note:**

When you type a phone number, the digits will automatically be grouped in the right order, including parentheses, dashes or no dashes as needed. The format used depends on the *Language & Region* settings in the *Settings* app.

A label is the name given to a field, such as 'home' for home phone. Sometimes a different notice appears here, such as 'home fax'. You can customize the label:

👉 **Tap** home

You see a list of labels from which to choose:

👉 **Tap** mobile

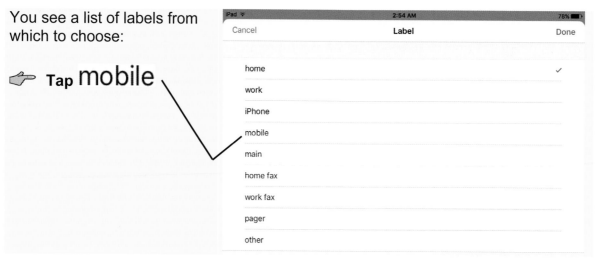

The label is changed. You can add a private number:

☞ **Tap** ⊕   add phone

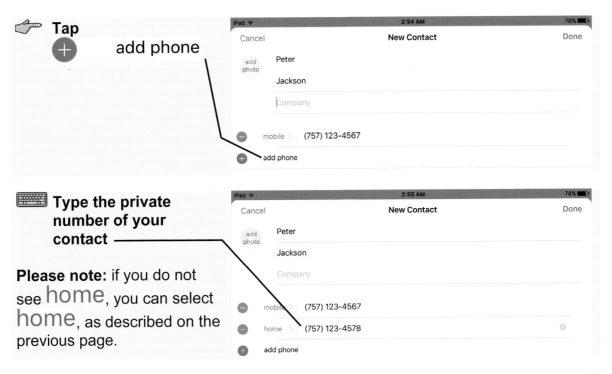

⌨ **Type the private number of your contact** ───────

Please note: if you do not see home, you can select home, as described on the previous page.

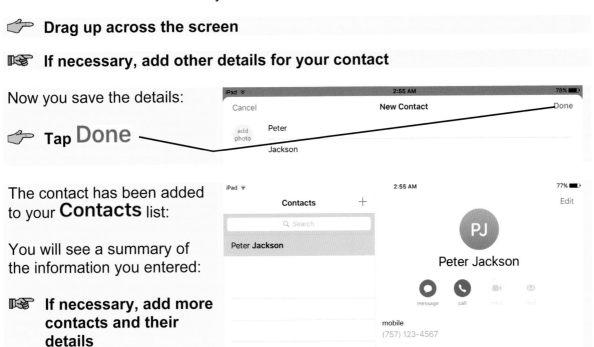

You can fill in more details for your contact. You decide how much information to add.

☞ **Drag up across the screen**

☞ **If necessary, add other details for your contact**

Now you save the details:

☞ **Tap Done** ───────

The contact has been added to your **Contacts** list:

You will see a summary of the information you entered:

☞ **If necessary, add more contacts and their details**

2.6 The Messages App

For sending a message you can use the *Messages* app. On the iPhone, it allows you to send an SMS or *iMessage* message. On the iPad, you can only use the *Messages* app for sending a text message if you have a mobile data plan with SIM card. You do however have the ability to send *iMessages* with your iPad to other users with an *Apple ID*. The screenshots in this section are made with an iPhone:

 Tap Messages

You see the *New Message* screen:

Type the first letter of the name of your contact

A list of contacts with the same first letter appears:

 Tap the desired contact

💡 **Tip**

Typing a telephone number or email address of an Apple ID

Instead of selecting a contact, by To: you can also type a phone number. The parentheses are automatically added. You can do the same with an email address. This only works if the receiver uses that email address as their *Apple ID*.

HELP! I see a different page.

If you previously sent or received messages, you will see a list of these messages here. You can then start a new message as follows:

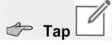 **Tap**

If necessary, you can add any additional recipients:

You do not need to do this now.

At the bottom of the screen:

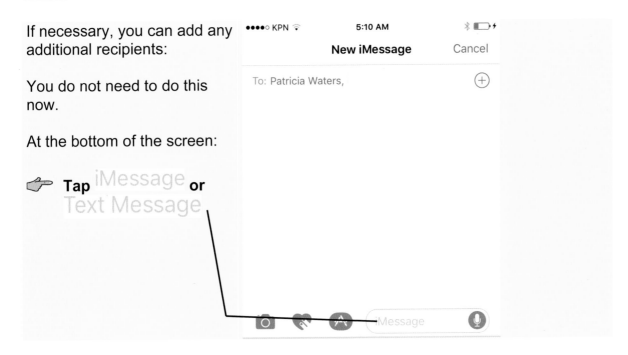

☞ **Tap** iMessage **or** Text Message

💡 Tip

SMS or iMessage

If you see Text Message, your message will be sent as an SMS and you may be charged a fee from your provider. If you see iMessage, this means the reciever has an iPhone, iPad or iPod Touch and *iMessage* is activated for both of you. Your message is then sent for free through the Internet, either with the use of a mobile data network (3G/4G) or with Wi-Fi. For 3G/4G you do have to pay the costs of data usage, but that is only about 140 bytes per message. The procedure for sending SMS and *iMessages* is the same.

⌨ **Type your message, for example:**

Hi Patricia, can I visit you at home tonight?

☞ **Tap** ⬆

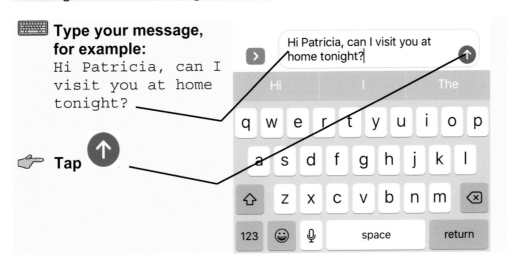

The message is sent:

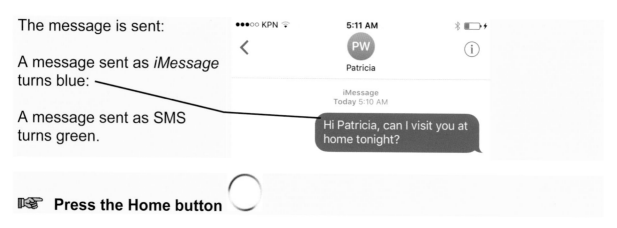

A message sent as *iMessage* turns blue:

A message sent as SMS turns green.

☞ **Press the Home button** ◯

If you receive an SMS or *iMessage* and the sound of your device is turned on, you will hear a sound signal.

If your device is in sleep mode, the screen lights up and you can read the message:

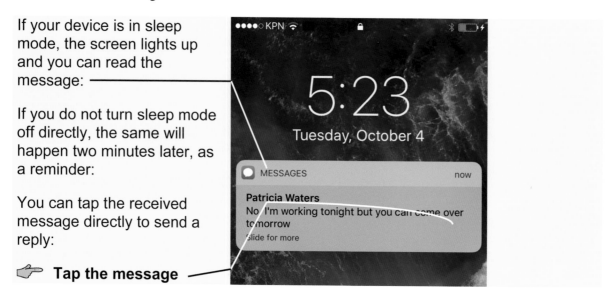

If you do not turn sleep mode off directly, the same will happen two minutes later, as a reminder:

You can tap the received message directly to send a reply:

☞ **Tap the message**

☞ **If necessary, give your passcode or use Touch ID to unlock your device**

You see the reply below your sent message:

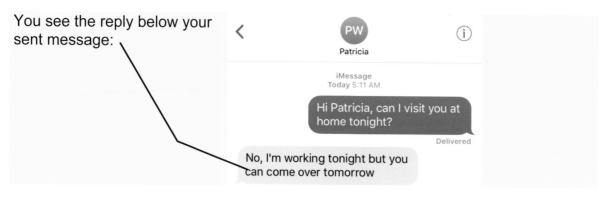

If you wait too long, or were away at the time, the notification will disappear. A new badge will then appear on top of the *Messages* app:

The number 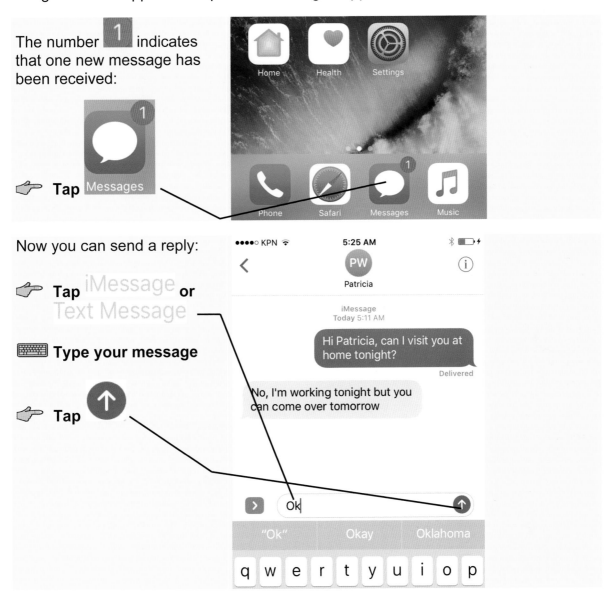 indicates that one new message has been received:

☞ **Tap** Messages

Now you can send a reply:

☞ **Tap** iMessage **or** Text Message

⌨ **Type your message**

☞ **Tap** ⬆

You can also delete a message. This may be convenient, for example, if you want to free up some memory space on your iPhone or iPad:

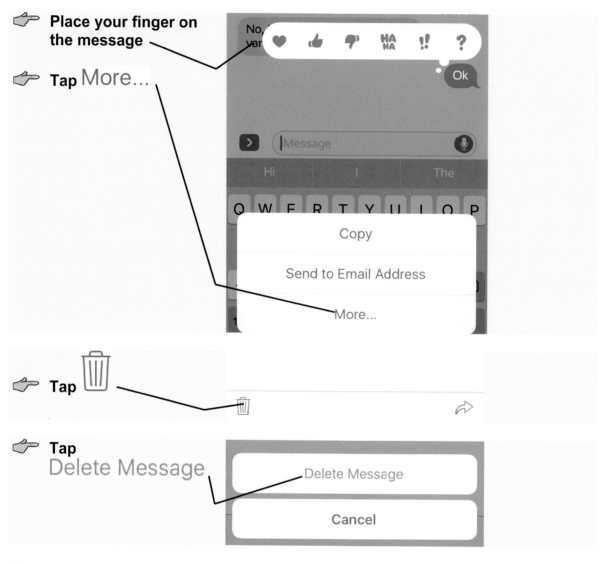

☞ **Place your finger on the message**

☞ **Tap** More...

☞ **Tap** 🗑

☞ **Tap** Delete Message

The message is deleted. You can also delete this person's entire conversation. For this you need to go back to the summary view of all the messages:

☞ **Tap** ‹

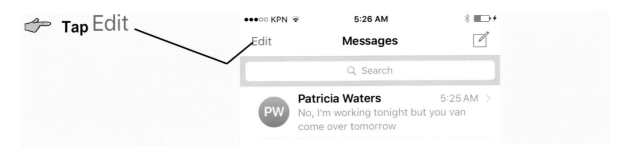

You select the conversation you want to delete:

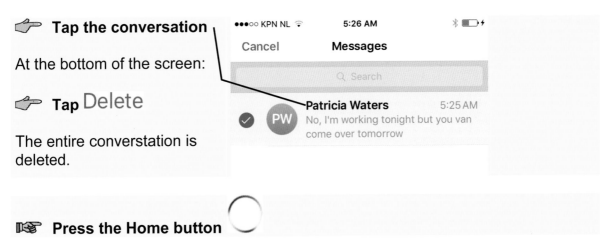

☞ **Tap the conversation**

At the bottom of the screen:

☞ **Tap** Delete

The entire converstation is deleted.

☞ **Press the Home button**

When you send a message to another iPhone, iPad or iPod Touch user, it automatically attempts to send your message with *iMessage*. This message is sent over the Internet, without having to pay SMS charges. You can view the *iMessage* settings:

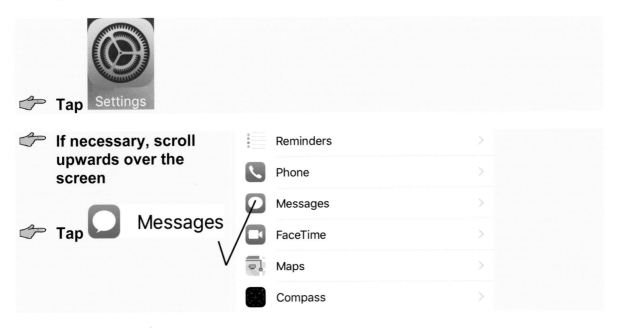

☞ **Tap** Settings

☞ **If necessary, scroll upwards over the screen**

☞ **Tap** Messages

iMessage is turned on:

If *iMessage* is turned off, tap by iMessage.

The button will then look like this .

☞ **Tap** ❮ Settings

💡 **Tip**

iMessages on all your Apple devices
If you want to look at your *iMessages* on all your Apple devices, such as an iPad, it is important that you use the same *Apple ID* on all these devices.

If you send a message, and in the text field you see iMessage instead of Text Message, your contact is also using *iMessage*. Your message will then automatically be sent as a free *iMessage*. You do not need to do anything. The procedures for sending an SMS or *iMessages* are the same.

☞ **Press the Home button**

2.7 Adding Bubble Animations

The *Messages* app has been greatly expanded in *iOS 10*. One of the most notable new features is the provision to add bubble like animations and effects to your messages, such as a question mark or a thumbs up icon 'to like' the message. By adding one of them, you can really liven up your messaging experience. A quick response can be sent to the person concerned, for example, with a thumbs up or heart icon added to it:

☞ **Tap** Messages

☞ **To see the list of messages, tap the name of a sender or a phone number**

A small bar appears with different options:

☞ **Press a message in the conversation and keep your finger briefly pressed**

☞ **Tap the desired option**

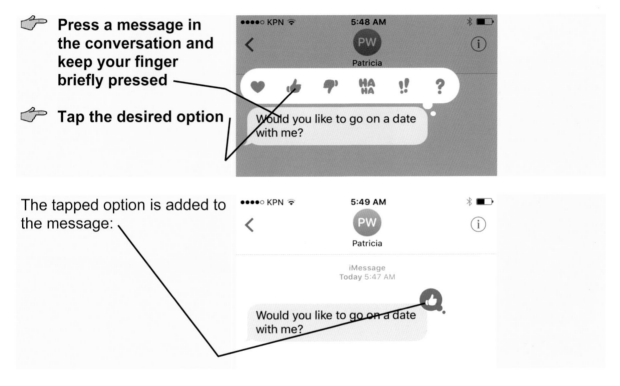

The tapped option is added to the message:

🖐 **Please note:**

These additions to messages are only visible for the recipients who have *iOS 10* or higher. On devices without this operating system, the recipients only see a text message without the extra icons.

At the end of this chapter you will find some more fun things to do with SMS in the *Tips,* such as replacing words quickly by emoji and adding effects to a message.

☞ **Press the Home button**

2.8 Message Notifications

The messages you receive are displayed in the *Notification Center*. From there you can read the message, but you can also reply to it directly:

As soon as your receive a message, a notification appears:

 **Tap the message**

The *Messages* app opens. You can answer the message if you want.

If your device was on stand-by when the message was received, you can also see a notification in the lock screen.

 **Unlock your device with Touch ID or passcode**

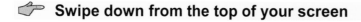 **Swipe down from the top of your screen**

By **Recent**, you will find the recently received messages by senders that have been added to your contact list. If the sender is not known, you will only see the telephone number:

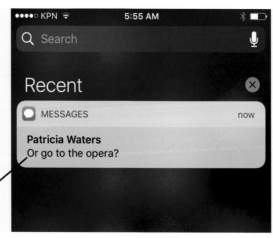

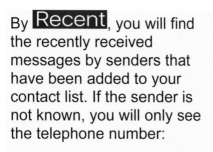 **Tap the message**

The *Messages* app opens. You can answer the message if you want. If you prefer not to see the notifications on the lock screen anymore, you can do as follows:

☞ **Swipe the message from right to left**

☞ **Tap Clear**

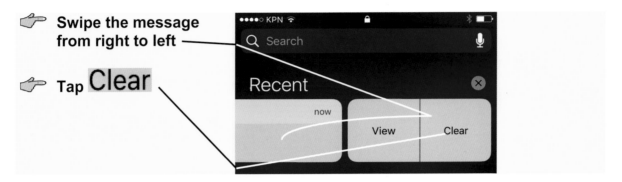

The message is deleted from the lock screen, but is still in the *Messages* app.

2.9 Calling

For calling you use the *Phone* app. You open *Phone* from the home screen of your iPhone:

☞ **If necessary, wake the iPhone out of sleep mode or turn it on**

At the bottom of the screen:

☞ **Tap Phone**

You dial the phone number of the person you wish to call:

👉 **If necessary, tap**

Keypad

⌨️ **Type the phone number**

At the top you see the number you will be dialing. The parentheses around the area code and the spaces are automatically added:

With ⊗ you can delete the numbers:

👉 **Tap**

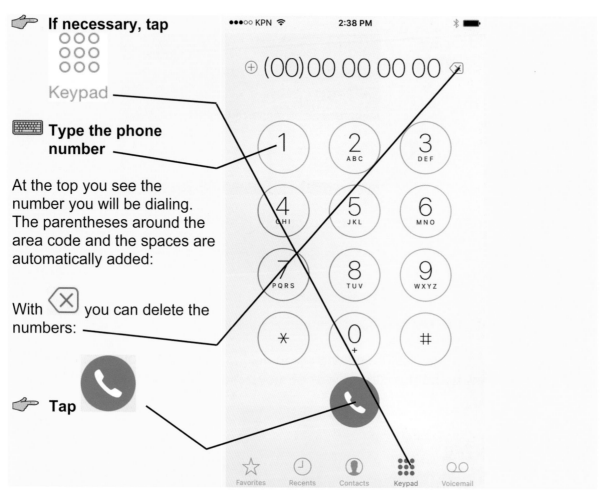

You can hear the telephone ring:

If you want to finish the call, you can briefly press the sleep/wake button on the side of your iPhone.

As soon as the person you call picks up, the calling time will be indicated here:

When the conversation is terminated, you can disconnect:

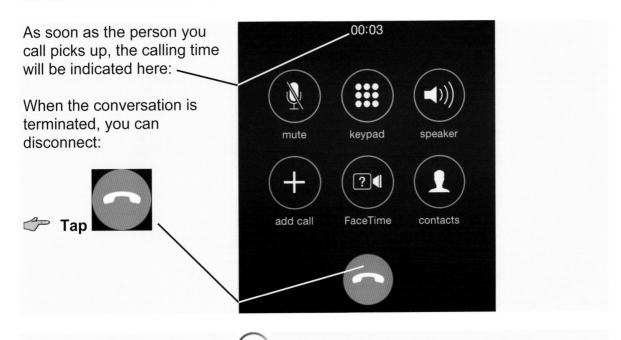

☞ **Tap**

Press the Home button

During a call, the screen will turn off when you hold the iPhone to your ear. Once you take the iPhone away from your ear, you will see a number of call options on the screen:

 Puts a conversation on hold.

 Brings the keys in view, so you can choose from a menu.

 Renders the call through a speaker.

 Initiates another phone call (while the other call is on hold).

 Starts a video call with *FaceTime* with the current caller. If a question mark appears on the button, *FaceTime* is not possible with this contact.

 Brings up the list of saved contacts, for example, to look up a phone number during the call.

If you receive a call yourself, you answer the call as follows. If the phone is still in sleep mode:

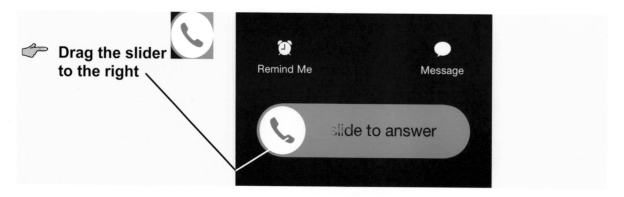

☞ **Drag the slider to the right**

If the phone is not in sleep mode:

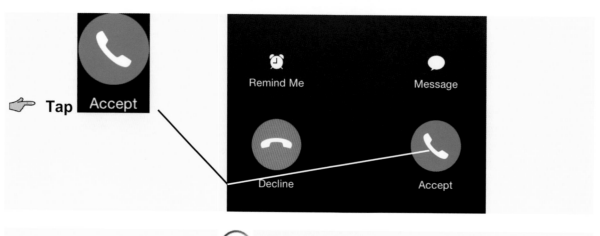

☞ **Tap** Accept

☞ **Press the Home button**

💡 **Tip**

Refusing a call

You can tap the Decline button to send an incoming call straight to your voicemail. This only works if your phone is not in sleep mode when the call comes in.

If your phone is in sleep mode, you can refuse a call as follows:

☞ **Press the sleep/wake button twice briefly**

2.10 Tips

 Tip

WhatsApp
A very popular alternative for chatting is the app called *WhatsApp*. With *WhatsApp* not only can you call and send text messages, you can share photos and videos as well. If Wi-Fi is turned on, you can call and send text messages with *WhatsApp* without any data charges. Another advantage is that *WhatsApp* is also available for other operating systems such as *Android* and *Windows*. So you can call and send text messages to non-iPhone users, as long as they have *WhatsApp* installed. Unfortunately *WhatsApp* is not available on the iPad.

 Tip

Reply to a WhatsApp message from the lock screen
A *WhatsApp* message will appear on the lock screen and *Notification Center,* just like a regular SMS. Below you can read how to respond to a message directly from the lock screen. The procedure for the *Notification Center* is the same.

☞ **Press the Home button**

In the lock screen, a notification of the message appears:

☞ **Swipe from left to right over the message**

☞ **Unlock your telephone via Touch ID or passcode**

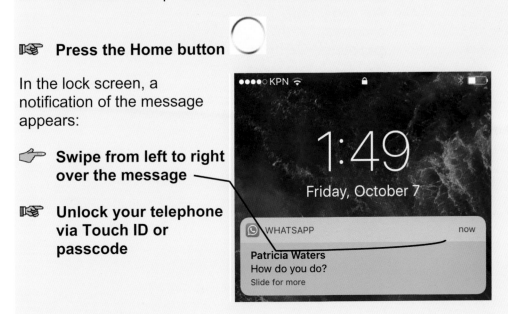

- Continue on the next page -

WhatsApp opens:

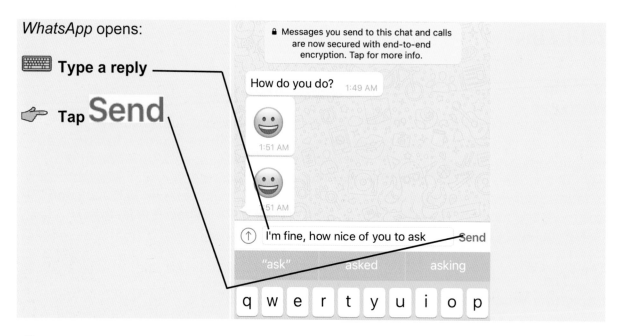

⌨ **Type a reply**

☞ **Tap Send**

Tip

Inserting emoji quickly in the Messages app

You can liven up an SMS or *iMessage* with emoji, drawn pictures representing people, animals, food, activities and more. *iOS 10* features a new, quick way to insert emoji:

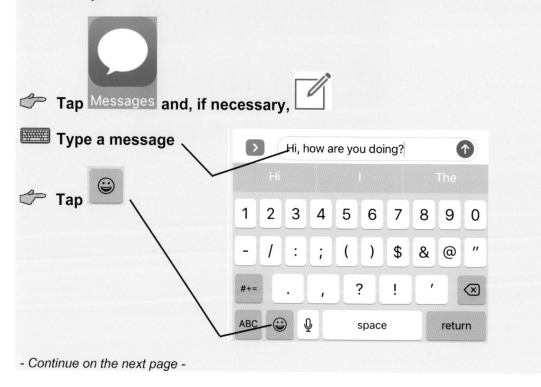

☞ **Tap Messages and, if necessary,** ✏️

⌨ **Type a message**

☞ **Tap** 😀

- Continue on the next page -

The words that are replacable by an emoji turn orange:

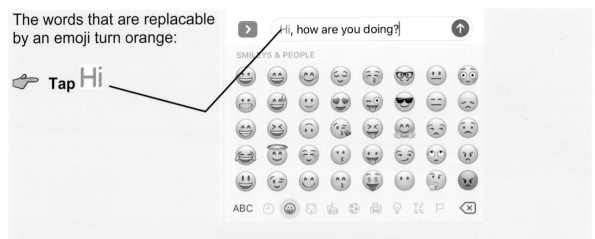

☞ **Tap** Hi

The word is automatically converted to the appropriate emoji like this:

👋|, how are you doing? . If there are several options, a bar is displayed, containing various appropriate emojis. You can click on an emoji to insert it, and then send the message in the usual way.

💡 **Tip**

Adding effects to a message

iOS 10 has another nice new feature in the *Messages* app. They can add a festive touch or a bit of life to your messages.

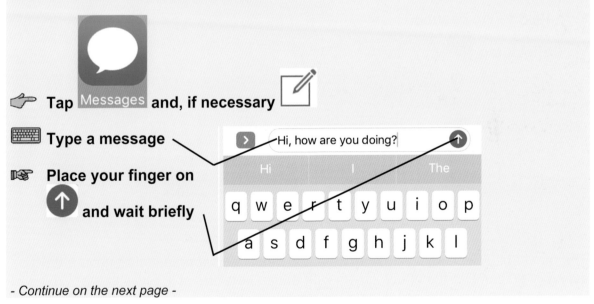

☞ **Tap** Messages **and, if necessary** ✏️

⌨ **Type a message**

☞ **Place your finger on** ↑ **and wait briefly**

- Continue on the next page -

A screen with possible effects appears:

INVISIBLE INK: makes the message 'unreadable'. By rubbing it, the message will become visible.

GENTLE: creates smaller letters.

LOUD: creates larger letters.

SLAM: provides the message with an animation.

To see these effects:

☞ **Next to the effect, tap**

To send the message:

☞ **Next to the desired**

effect, tap ⬆

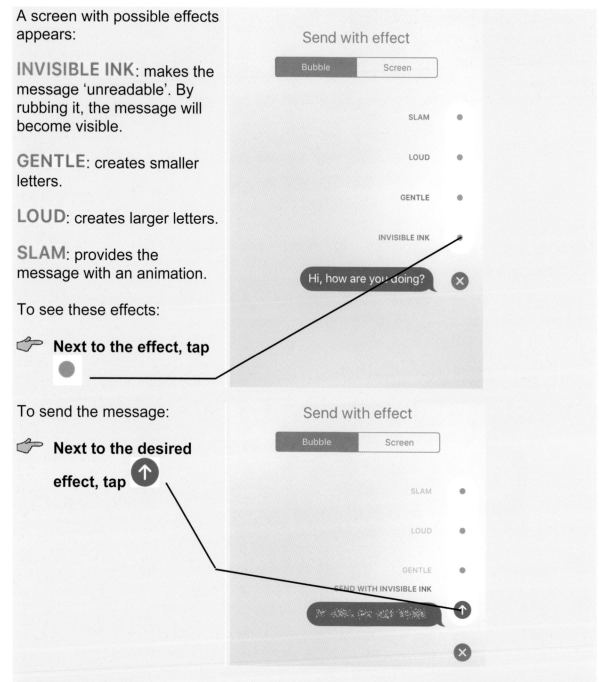

The message will be sent with your selected effect. Only persons that have a device with *iOS 10* can see the effect. Users with earlier versions of *iOS* will see a text message alluding to the effect that was meant, such as 'sent with invisible ink'.

- Continue on the next page -

It is also possible to send an animation combined with your message. For this you can repeat the steps from the previous page up to the point that the different effects appear:

👉 **Tap**

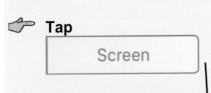

You can see an animation with balloons:

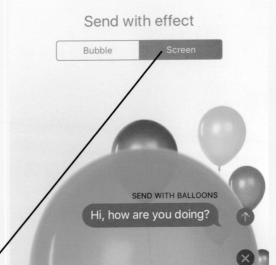

Different animations are available:

To see all the effects:

👉 **Swipe from left to right**

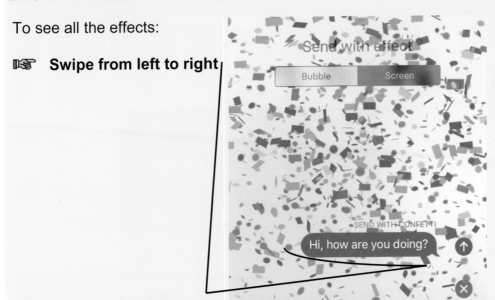

There are animations with balloons, confetti, laser, fireworks and falling stars in *iOS 10*. If you see a nice effect, just give it a try. Tap to add the animation to the message.

👉 **Tap**

The message will be sent, with your selected effect. Again only persons that have a device with *iOS 10* can see the effect. Users with earlier versions of *iOS* will see a text message alluding to the effect that was meant, such as 'sent with shooting star'.

Tip

Drawing messages with your fingers

In the *Messages* app you can send a drawing or handwritten message to other users with *iOS 10*:

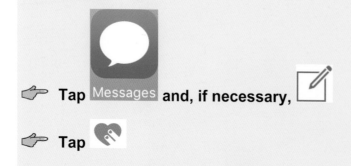

☞ **Tap** Messages **and, if necessary,** 🖉

☞ **Tap** 💗

If you do not see the icon, tap 〉.

At the bottom of the screen a new section appears with some miniature icons for the features that are available for drawing. First, you can expand this window to work more easily:

☞ **Tap** ⌃

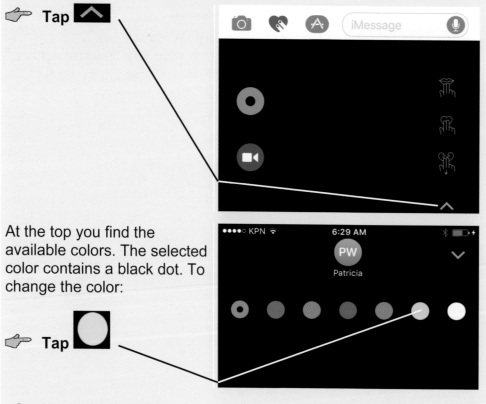

At the top you find the available colors. The selected color contains a black dot. To change the color:

☞ **Tap** ⬤

- Continue on the next page -

To make a drawing or handwrite a word:

☞ **Move your finger over the black area**

To send the drawing:

👉 **Tap**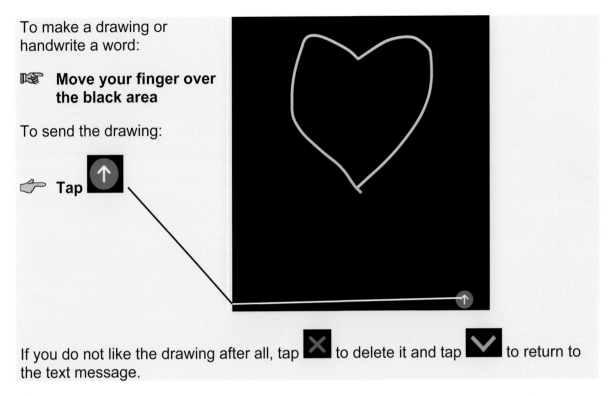

If you do not like the drawing after all, tap ❌ to delete it and tap ✅ to return to the text message.

💡 **Tip**

Setting up an email account of your Internet service provider

In this *Tip* you can read how to set up an email account for your own Internet service provider, such as Charter, Comcast, Cox, AT & T, EarthLink or Verizon. To do this, you will need the information about the incoming and outgoing mail server, the user name and password given to you by your provider.

👉 **Tap** Settings

On the left-hand side of the screen:

👉 **Tap** ✉ Mail

👉 **Tap** Accounts

- Continue on the next page -

☞ **Tap** Add Account

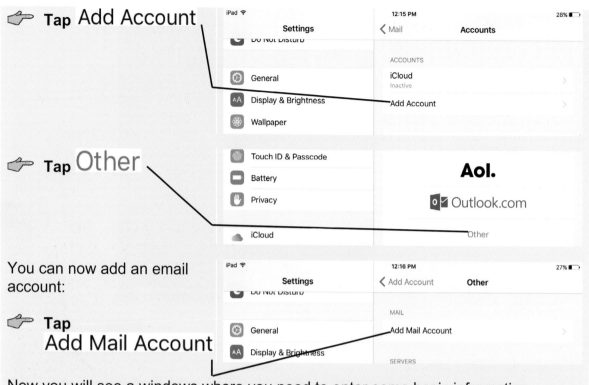

☞ **Tap** Other

You can now add an email account:

☞ **Tap** Add Mail Account

Now you will see a windows where you need to enter some basic information concerning your email account.

⌨ **By** Name**, type your name**

⌨ **By** Email**, enter your email address**

⌨ **By** Password**, type your password**

⌨ **By** Description**, type an identifiable name for your email account**

When you have finished entering the information:

☞ **Tap** Next

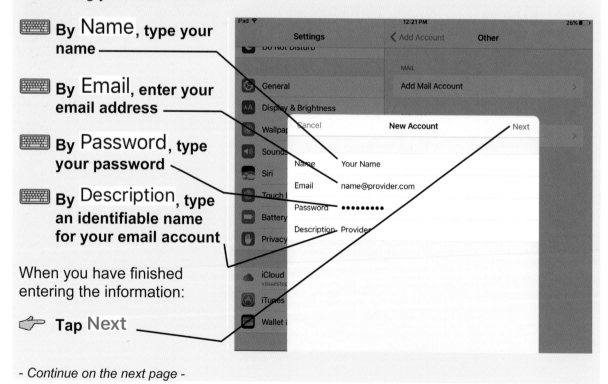

- Continue on the next page -

Now you can select whether you want to set up your email account as an *IMAP* or a *POP* account:

- IMAP stands for *Internet Message Access Protocol*. This means that you will manage your messages on the mail server. Messages that have been read will be stored on the mail server, until you delete them. IMAP is useful if you manage your emails from multiple devices. Your mailbox will look the same on each device. When you create folders for organizing your email messages, you will see the same folders on other devices as well as your iPad or iPhone. If you want to use IMAP, you will need to set up your email account as an IMAP account on all the other devices that you use.
- POP stands for *Post Office Protocol*, the traditional way of managing email. When you retrieve your messages, they will immediately be deleted from the server. Although, on your iPad the default setting for POP accounts is for a copy to be stored on the server, after you have retrieved a message. This means you will still be able to retrieve the message on your other computers or devices.

☞ Tap POP or IMAP

By INCOMING MAIL SERVER:

⌨ By Host Name,
type the name of the incoming mail server

⌨ By User Name,
type the user name

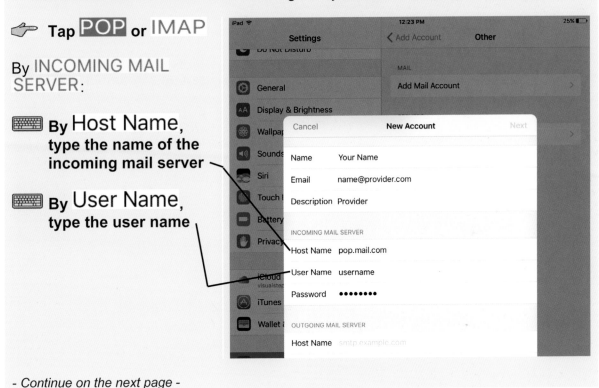

- Continue on the next page -

☞ **Drag your finger upwards a bit, on the screen**

By OUTGOING MAIL SERVER:

⌨ By Host Name, **type the name of the outgoing mail server**

If by OUTGOING MAIL SERVER you see the text Optional in the fields for the user name and password, you do not need to enter this information.

☞ **Tap** Next

☞ **Tap** Save

Now your email account has been added:

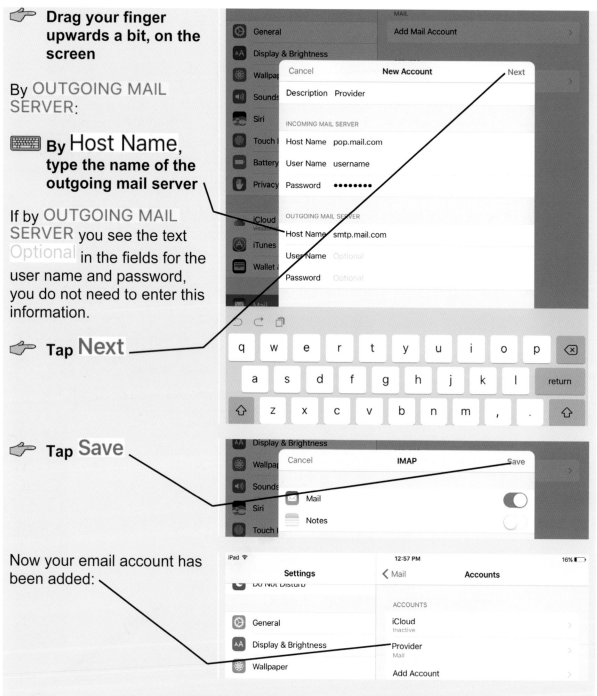

Are you having difficulty setting up your email account? With the growing popularity of the iPad and the iPhone, many providers such as AT&T and AOL have put instructions on their websites about setting up an email account for the iPad or iPhone. Just look for something like 'email settings iPad' of 'email settings iPhone' on your provider's website and follow the given instructions.

3. Apps

Apps are one of the core features of the iPad and iPhone. What is new in *iOS 10* is the increased role of widgets, handy apps that give you quick access to information. In this chapter, you will learn more about these widgets, where you can find them and how to add or remove them.

Some of the standard apps, such as *Stocks* or *Weather*, can be hidden in *iOS 10*, so you have more space on the screen for the apps you use regularly. In previous versions, this was not possible.

Safari, Apple's standard browsing app, lets you surf the Internet. You can browse multiple websites using various tabs and access your favorite websites easily. The *Maps* app will get you even more quickly to your destination. Planning your route is much improved with the brighter colors and crisper text in the *iOS 10* version of the app.

In the *App Store* you can download new apps. To work simultaneously in multiple applications, the features *Split View* and *Slide Over* come in handy.

You can switch on voice assistant *Siri* to help you answer questions, and *Spotlight* helps you to locate information quickly on your iPad or iPhone, or on the Internet and Wikipedia. For syncing and storing important information online, you can use *iCloud*, Apple's storage service.

In this chapter you learn how to:

- open and use widgets;
- add, sort and delete widgets;
- delete (standard) apps;
- surf with *Safari*;
- open new tabs;
- add a website to your list of favorites;
- search for locations and plan your route with the *Maps* app*;*
- download apps in the *App Store*;
- switch between apps;
- use *Split View* and *Slide Over*;
- sort apps and save them in folders;
- work with *Siri and Spotlight*;
- turn on *iCloud*.

3.1 Widgets

Widgets are tools for getting access to information quickly without the need of opening an app. In *iOS 10* the widgets are prominent in the *Notification Center*. You can use the standard widgets, but also add additional widgets. Widgets that you do not use (anymore), you can remove.
By default, there are a number of widgets that can be seen in the *Notification Center*. The iPad and iPhone do not show the same widgets. In total there are eighteen different widgets available. To open the default widgets:

☞ **Unlock your iPad or iPhone with Touch ID or a passcode**

☞ **Swipe from left to right over the screen**

 HELP! I do not see the Notification Center.
If you do not see the *Notification Center*, but only a list of apps, then you are probably viewing one of the other pages of the home screen. If necessary, swipe from left to right over the screen. You will automatically arrive at the first page, and if you swipe again, you will see the *Notification Center*.

You see a number of standard widgets vertically in a row:

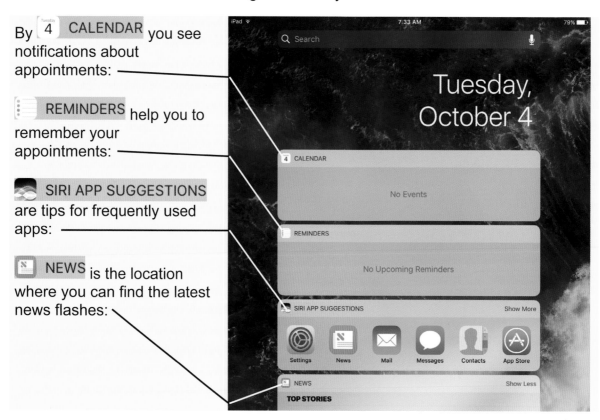

By 4 CALENDAR you see notifications about appointments: ─────

📋 REMINDERS help you to remember your appointments: ─────

🏔 SIRI APP SUGGESTIONS are tips for frequently used apps: ─────

📰 NEWS is the location where you can find the latest news flashes: ─────

You can open the widgets and view the content. For example, take a closer look at the  NEWS widget:

☞ **Tap a news flash**

The referring site or app where the news was published will open.

To return to the widgets:

☞ **Press the Home button**

☞ **Swipe from left to right over the screen**

These widgets are still available:

Activity	People with an Apple Watch can see here how active they are.
Favorites	A list of favorite contacts. Convenient way to quickly call them or send a message.
Mail	With this widget you can quickly open the messages from your favorite contacts.
Maps Destinations	Shows traffic information about your frequently used routes or about the appointments in your calendar.
Maps Nearby	A map with locations in your vicinity. The map changes during different moments in the day.
Maps Transit	Public transport information. Not available in all countries.
Music	A list of recently created playlists.
Notes	Open your recently created notes.
Tips	Tips for using *iOS 10*.

To close the list of widgets:

☞ **Press the Home button**

3.2 Adding Widgets

By default, a number of widgets are already shown in the *Notification Center*. You can add widgets to the list yourself:

☞ **Unlock your device with Touch ID or passcode**

☞ **Swipe from the left to the right**

☞ **Drag up from the bottom of the screen**

☞ **Tap**

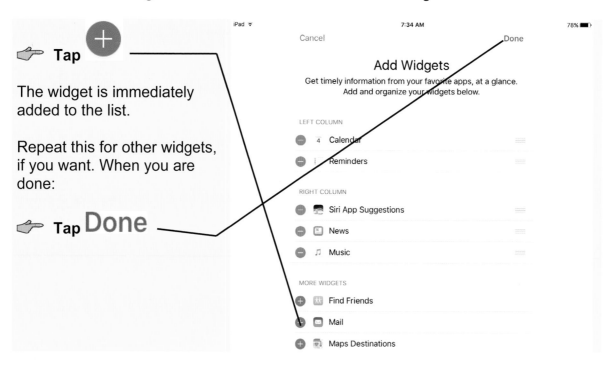

In the menu that appears, widgets that are shown will have a ⊖ button next to their name. The notification about 'left column' and 'right column' you can ignore. The other available widgets are below these ones. To add a widget:

☞ **Tap** ⊕

The widget is immediately added to the list.

Repeat this for other widgets, if you want. When you are done:

☞ **Tap Done**

The widget(s) are now inserted in the *Notification Center* at the bottom of the list.

3.3 Sorting and Deleting Widgets

It is also possible to rearrange or delete widgets. Rearranging goes like this:

☞ **Unlock your iPad or iPhone with Touch ID or a passcode**

☞ **Swipe from the left to the right over the screen**

☞ **Drag up from the bottom of the screen**

☞ **Tap** Edit

The widgets with a 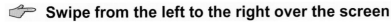 to the left of the name can be moved up or down. They will be subsequently shown in a different order in the *Notification Center*.

☞ **Place your finger next to the desired widget on**

☞ **Press gently and slide your finger up or down to change the order**

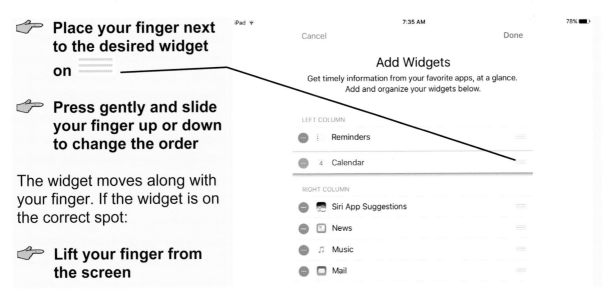

The widget moves along with your finger. If the widget is on the correct spot:

☞ **Lift your finger from the screen**

It is also possible to remove a widget, so that it no longer appears in the *Notification Center*. This actually only deactivates the widget, they are not deleted from your iPad or iPhone, but simply not displayed anymore. To remove a widget, you first open the *Notification Center* in the manner described above:

☞ **Tap**

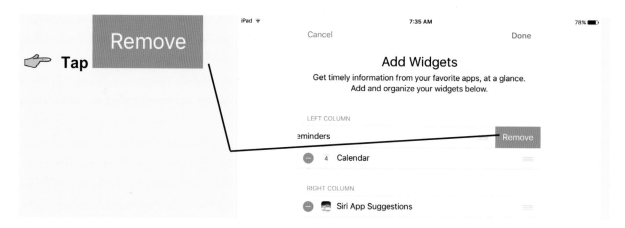

The widget disappears from the top list and returns to the section below, where all the still available widgets are displayed.

☞ Tap Done

☞ Press the Home button ⬭

3.4 Removing (Standard) Apps

Standard apps are those apps every user has on his iPad or iPhone by default. These apps were not removable all the way through the *iOS 9* version. This annoyed many people. They thought it should be up to the user to decide which apps can or cannot be used, and not to Apple. Apple has taken the criticism to heart in *iOS 10*. A number of standard apps are finally removable in *iOS 10*. They are then no longer visible on your device, and are not displayed by default alongside other apps.

The apps you now can remove are: *Stocks, Calculator, Contacts, Voice Memos, FaceTime, Reminders, Home, iBooks, iCloud Drive, iTunes Store, Maps, Calendar, Compass, Mail, Music, News, Notes, Podcasts, Tips, Videos, Watch, Weather* and *Find Friends*. Not all of these apps are available on both the iPad or iPhone. For example, you can find *Stocks* only on iPhones.

So you can now delete apps from your iPad or iPhone. These might even be the apps you have downloaded yourself. Downloading apps is explained later in this chapter in *section 3.10 Downloading and Installing Apps.*

**Place your finger on
one of the apps** ——

 By the desired app,

tap ⊗

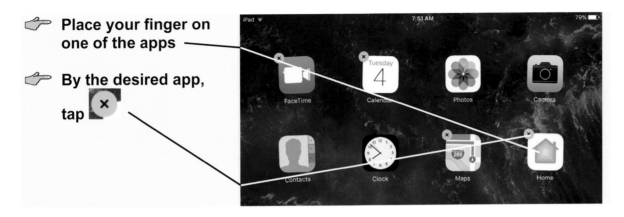

If you are sure you want to remove the app:

 Tap Remove

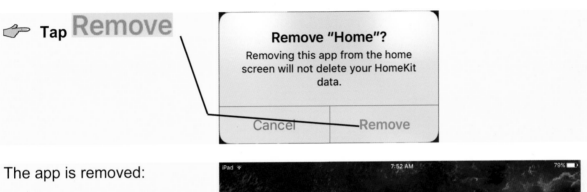

> **Remove "Home"?**
> Removing this app from the home
> screen will not delete your HomeKit
> data.
>
> Cancel | Remove

The app is removed:

 Press the Home button

Please note:

If you hide these apps, you will not see them on the home screen anymore. They can therefore not be used either. If you hide the *Contacts* app for example, this may prove to be inconvenient. So only hide the apps you really do not use. The apps you have hidden before, must be made visible again before you can use them.

To unhide the app, you must download them again from the *App Store*. In *section 3.10 Downloading and Installing Apps* you will learn how to download an app.

3.5 Navigating in Safari

The standard web browser for surfing the Internet is *Safari*. You can open a new web page in *Safari* as follows:

At the bottom of the screen:

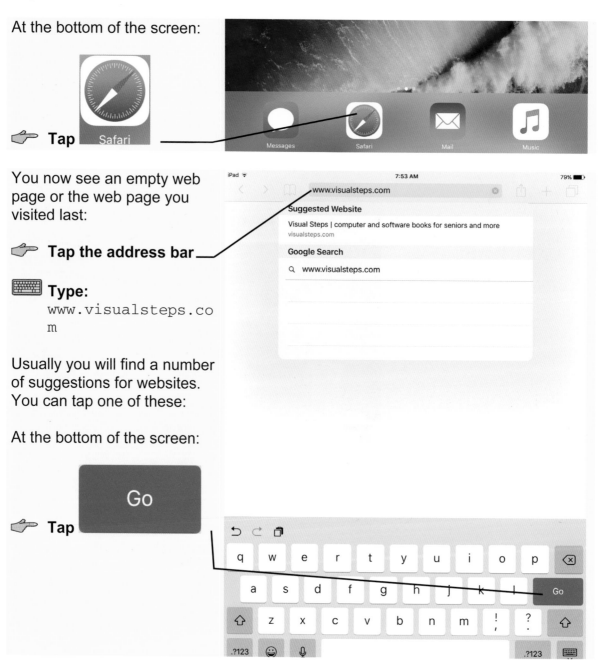

☞ **Tap** Safari

You now see an empty web page or the web page you visited last:

☞ **Tap the address bar**

⌨ **Type:**
www.visualsteps.co m

Usually you will find a number of suggestions for websites. You can tap one of these:

At the bottom of the screen:

☞ **Tap** Go

If you look at a website on your iPhone or iPad, the letters and images are often too small to be able to read them. You can zoom in on the iPad and iPhone by double-tapping:

☞ **Double-tap the menu on the left**

To zoom out again:

☞ **Double-tap the menu again**

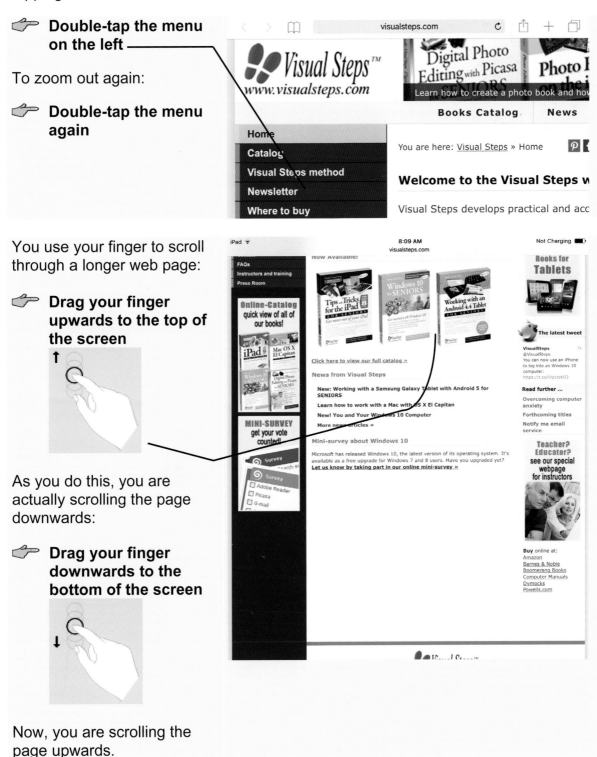

You use your finger to scroll through a longer web page:

☞ **Drag your finger upwards to the top of the screen**

As you do this, you are actually scrolling the page downwards:

☞ **Drag your finger downwards to the bottom of the screen**

Now, you are scrolling the page upwards.

Tip

Scrolling sideways
You can also scroll sideways on a page by moving your finger from right to left, or from left to right over the screen.

On long pages it can be irritating if you want to return to the top of the page and have to use quite a number of swipes to get there. Fortunately, this can be done easier:

☞ **Double-tap the status bar**

If a page contains a link (also called hyperlink), you can open it by simply tapping it:

☞ **Double-tap the menu**

☞ **Tap** **Catalog**

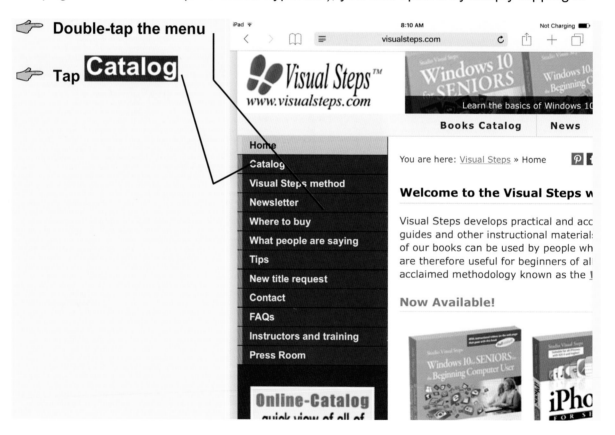

The page of the tapped link now appears. If you want to return to the page you saw earlier, tap ⟨ at the top of the screen.

3.6 Opening New Tabs

As you are surfing the Internet it can be useful to open a hyperlink in another tab. This way the site you are currently on will remain open. The tapped link will open in a new tab. So now you have two pages at your disposal:

☞ **Place your finger on** **Visual Steps method**

After a few moments a menu appears:

☞ **Tap** **Open in New Tab**

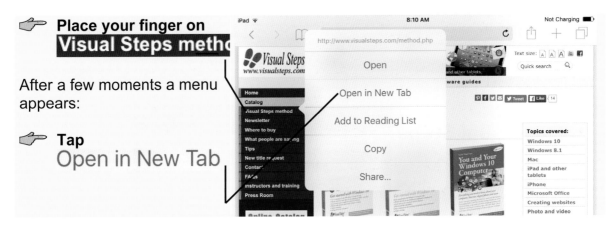

The tab opens on the right-hand side of the active tab on your iPad. To open another tab:

☞ **Tap the title of the tab, for example** **The Visual Steps Met**

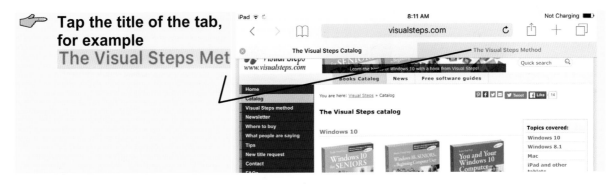

If many tabs are open, they will not be completely visible. You can scroll through the tabs by swiping your finger over the tabs left to right or vice versa. The hidden tabs will then be displayed. By tapping a tab, it will open.

You can close a tab that is open like this:

In the tab section:

☞ **Tap the desired tab**

On your iPhone the tabs are organized a little differently. If you open a link in a new tab, automatically a new tab will open. To close a tab:

At the bottom of the screen:

☞ Tap

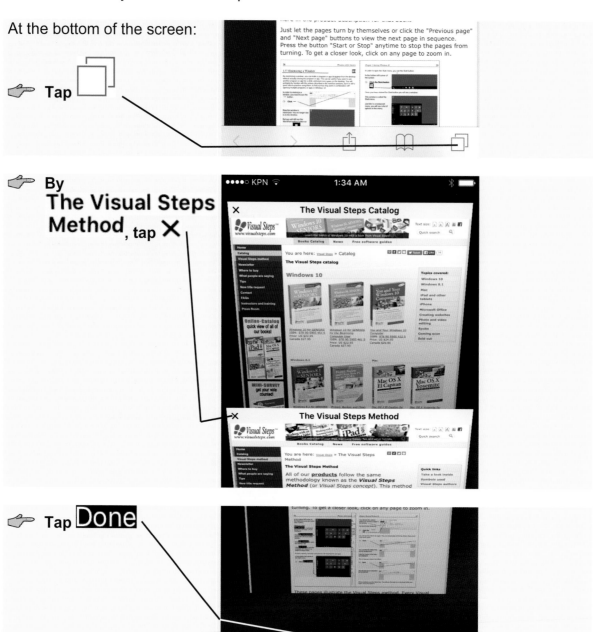

☞ By **The Visual Steps Method**, tap ✕

☞ Tap **Done**

3.7 Saving Your Favorite Websites

Favorite websites can be saved in *Safari* in the so-called *Favorites* folder. You can sort them into subfolders too, to allow for a more compact overview. To learn how to save a website as a favorite, go back to the home page for the Visual Steps website:

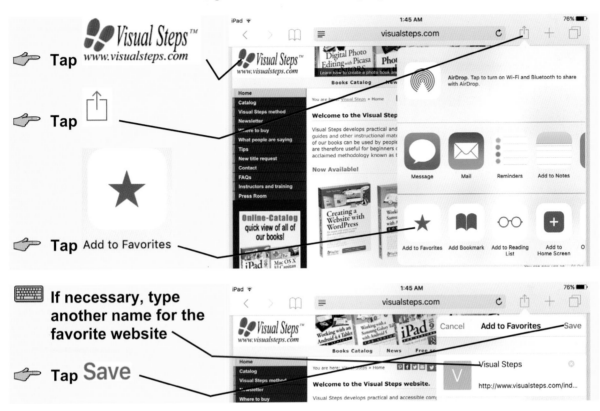

☞ **Tap** www.visualsteps.com

☞ **Tap** [share icon]

☞ **Tap** Add to Favorites

⌨ **If necessary, type another name for the favorite website**

☞ **Tap** Save

The favorite website is now stored. Here is how to view your stored favorites:

☞ **Tap** [bookmark icon]

☞ **Tap** ☆ Favorites

You see the stored favorites. It is a good idea to use folders and subfolders for websites covering the same topic. For instance, you could have a folder named Recipes and a subfolder named Dinner. Here is how to create a new (sub)folder:

At the bottom of the screen:

☞ **Tap** Edit

☞ **Tap** New Folder

You give the new folder a name:

Type: Example

On the keyboard:

Done

Tap

Next, you move the favorite to the new folder:

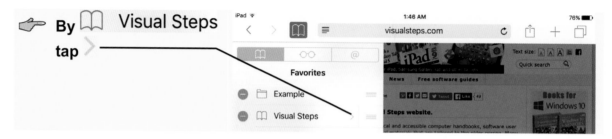

By 📖 **Visual Steps**

tap ❯

You see the window *Edit Bookmark*:

The favorite is currently
stored in the *Favorites* folder:

Tap ☆ **Favorites**

You can choose the new folder:

Tap 📁 **Example**

Tap ❮ **Favorites**

The favorite is moved to the *Example* folder: ─────────

At the bottom of the screen:

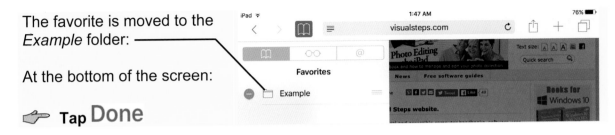

☞ **Tap** Done

You can close the window with favorites:

☞ **Tap** 📖

☞ **Press the Home button** ⭕

💡 **Tip**
Removing a folder or a favorite
You can remove a folder with favorites as follows:

☞ **Tap** 📖, Edit

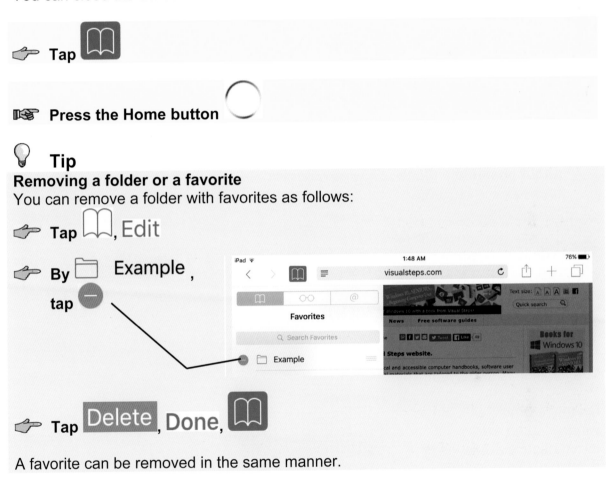

☞ **By** 📁 **Example**,

tap ➖

☞ **Tap** Delete, Done, 📖

A favorite can be removed in the same manner.

3.8 The Maps App

The *Maps* app allows you to search for locations, find places for doing things or plan a route to a destination. It is also possible to navigate with it as an alternative to the GPS in your car or on your bike.

Looking up a location in *Maps* can be done in a heartbeat:

☞ **Tap** Maps

Maps asks for your location the first time you use it. This is convenient, because searching for locations in your immediate vicinity can be done more quickly.

☞ **Tap** Allow

The app opens. You can look for a location:

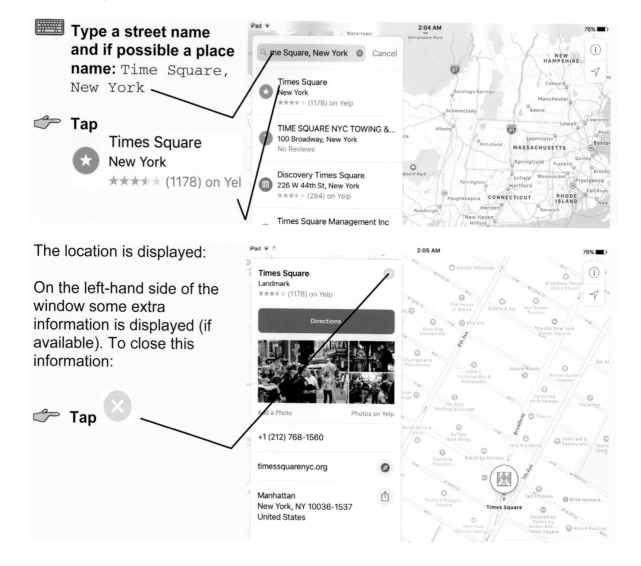

⌨ **Type a street name and if possible a place name:** Time Square, New York

☞ **Tap**

⭐ Times Square
New York
★★★☆☆ (1178) on Yel

The location is displayed:

On the left-hand side of the window some extra information is displayed (if available). To close this information:

☞ **Tap** ✕

The map will remain in view but the pin with the location is gone. You can zoom in and out on the map:

☞ **Move your thumb and index finger away from each other on the screen**

The map is enlarged. To zoom in:

☞ **Move your thumb and index finger towards each other on the screen**

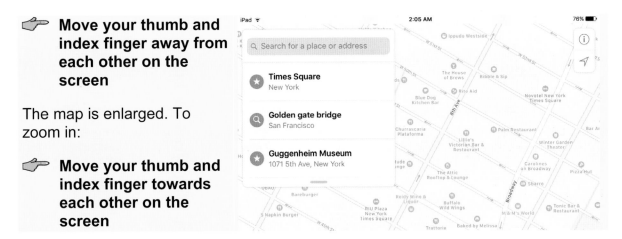

3.9 Planning Your Route with the Maps App

Do you want to plan a route from your current location to a particular street or location?

☞ Tap **Directions**

☞ The first time you see a warning notice:

☞ Tap OK

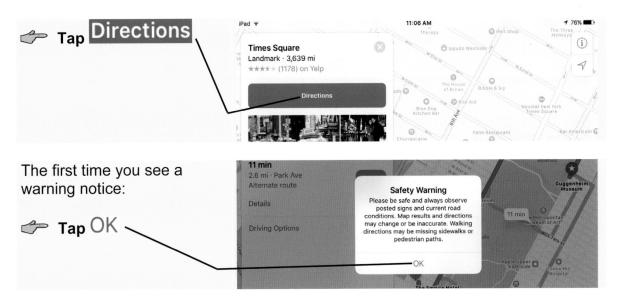

Possible routes may appear. You see the fastest route and one or more alternatives. The quickest route is marked dark blue. Alternative routes are light blue. Tap one of the alternative routes to see how it is displayed on the map in dark blue, and to be able to select it.

By default, the route for car traffic is displayed. At the bottom of the screen you can

also choose for Walk or Transit. To use this route as navigation while you drive:

Similar to navigational devices from Garmin or TomTom, *Maps* shows you the way step by step. To return to the main menu:

The address you just looked for is now in the search field.

By default, the *Maps* app plans the route from your current location to your final destination. You can also choose a different point of departure:

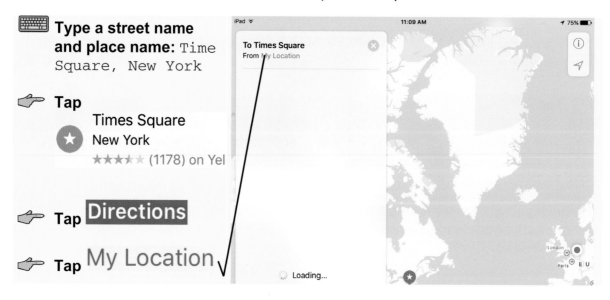

Type a different street name and place name: Empire State Building

☞ **Tap** **Empire State Building** 350 5th Ave, New York · ★★★★ (1518) on Yelp

☞ **Tap** Route

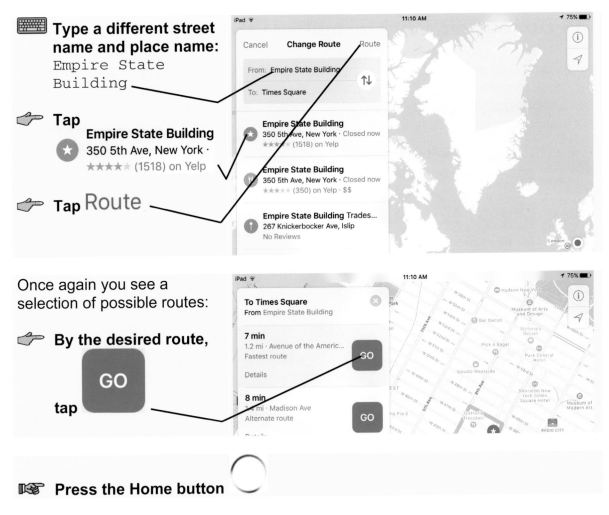

Once again you see a selection of possible routes:

☞ **By the desired route,** tap **GO**

 Press the Home button

Please note:

Maps uses your GPS and Internet connection. Please be aware that this may affect the data use on your iPhone or iPad, especially if you want to use this feature when traveling abroad.

Tip

Planning your public transport route

In the United States, *iOS 10* makes it possible to find public transportation routes in the *Maps* app as well. This feature is only available in a few major cities across the United States, but in the future there will be more added.

3.10 Downloading and Installing Apps

In the *App Store* you can find thousands of apps that you can use on your iPad and iPhone. A number of these can be downloaded for free. In this section you can read how to download a free app. To download a paid app, you need to add payment information to your account. This is not discussed in this book. To access the *App Store*:

☞ **Tap** App Store

The *App Store* might ask the first time for access to your location. If you do not want this:

☞ **Tap** Don't Allow

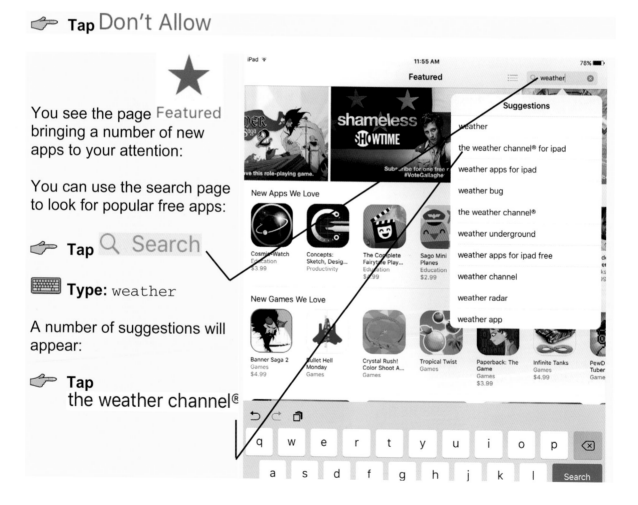

You see the page Featured bringing a number of new apps to your attention:

You can use the search page to look for popular free apps:

☞ **Tap** 🔍 Search

⌨ **Type:** weather

A number of suggestions will appear:

☞ **Tap**
   the weather channel®

The page with the app is displayed:

If necessary, you can also
display a page with additional
information about the app, by
tapping the image:

You can download the app:

👉 **Tap** [GET]

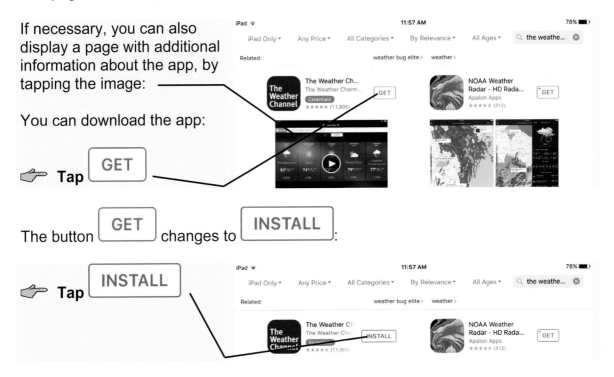

The button [GET] changes to [INSTALL]:

👉 **Tap** [INSTALL]

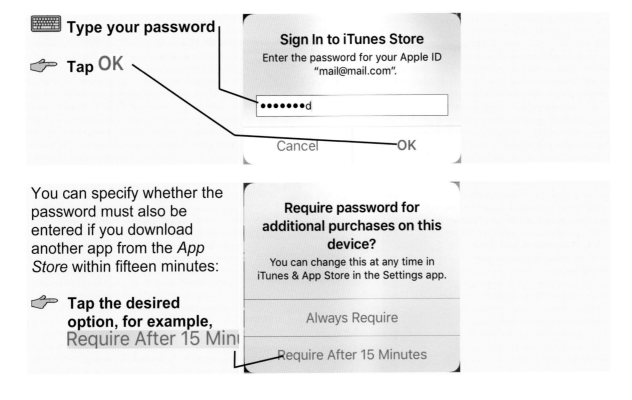

Before the app is installed, you have to sign in with your *Apple ID*:

⌨ **Type your password**

👉 **Tap OK**

> **Sign In to iTunes Store**
> Enter the password for your Apple ID
> "mail@mail.com".
>
> [•••••••d]
>
> Cancel   OK

You can specify whether the
password must also be
entered if you download
another app from the *App
Store* within fifteen minutes:

👉 **Tap the desired
option, for example,**
Require After 15 Min

> **Require password for
> additional purchases on this
> device?**
> You can change this at any time in
> iTunes & App Store in the Settings app.
>
> Always Require
>
> Require After 15 Minutes

The app is installed when you see the button OPEN :

You do not have to open the app now.

☞ **Press the Home button**

3.11 Switching Between Apps

If more apps are opened, you can go quickly to the desired app. In the previous sections you already opened a couple of apps.

☞ **Swipe up over the screen with four or five fingers at once**

You will see a screen like this:

You can tap the desired app to reopen it:

☞ **Tap the window of the** *App Store*

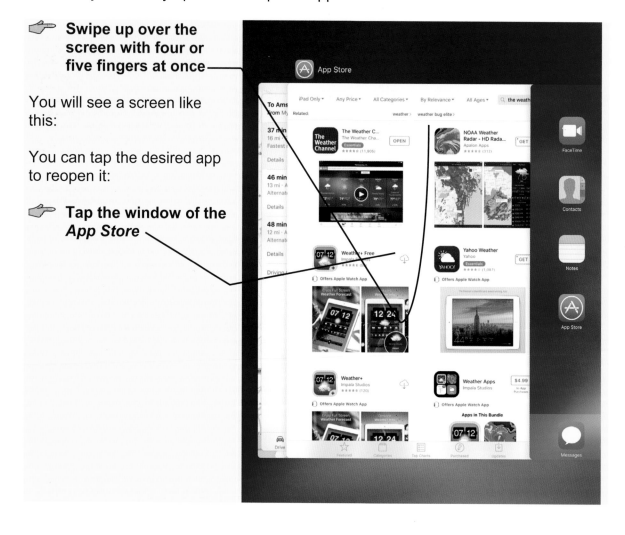

You can also open this screen by pressing the Home button twice quickly.

☞ **Press the Home button twice quickly**

👉 **Swipe from right to left over the screen** ——

The home screen is always the last app on the right-hand side.

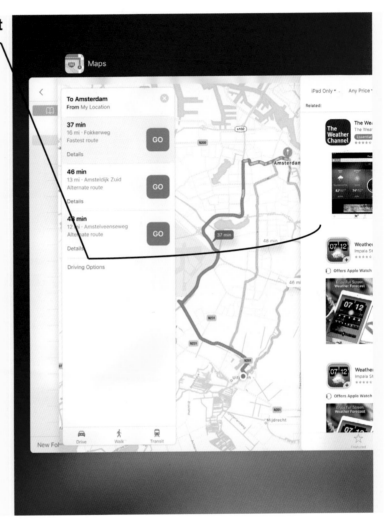

In this way you can close an app you are no longer using, for example the *App Store*:

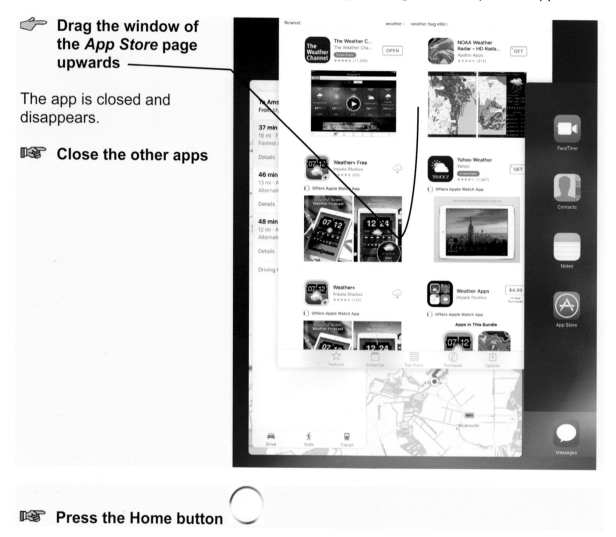

☞ **Drag the window of the *App Store* page upwards**

The app is closed and disappears.

☞ **Close the other apps**

☞ **Press the Home button**

3.12 Slide Over and Split View

With the *Slide Over* feature you can open a second app in a narrow panel on the right-hand side of your screen. The other app is dimmed and in waiting mode, which allows you to switch over quickly. This is useful when you are surfing and for example just want to check your email.

For the best view of *Slide Over* hold the iPad in landscape mode. On the iPhone, this option is not available.

☞ **Turn the iPad to a horizontal position**

☞ **Tap** Safari

☞ **Swipe your screen from right to left**

If you use *Slide Over* for the first time or use it after a long time of inactivity, you must choose which app you want to use by default for the *Slide Over* feature. On the right, a selection bar appears with different apps to choose from. By swiping up and down you can browse this list. If you have used *Slide Over* before on your iPad, you see the app that was last used for *Slide Over*.

☞ **Drag up and down over the right-hand side until you see the *Maps* app**

☞ **Tap** Maps

Both apps are open and active. They can be used at the same time:

This is called *Split View*.

If you want to replace the second app for another app, you can do this as follows:

☞ **Drag** ▬▬ **down**

☞ **If necessary, drag the list up or down**

☞ **Tap the desired app, for example** *Reminders*

To close *Split View:*

☞ **Tap the left app**

You see the first app in full view.

☞ **Press the Home button**

☞ **Turn the iPad to a vertical position**

➙ **Please note:**
Apps from other developers than Apple may not be suitable for *Split View* and *Slide Over*. This is why you do not see all of your apps in the list.

3.13 Sorting and Storing Apps in Folders

The order of apps on your iPad and iPhone can completely be customized to your own requirements by rearranging them. Your installed apps can be found on the second home screen:

☞ **Swipe from left to right on the home screen**

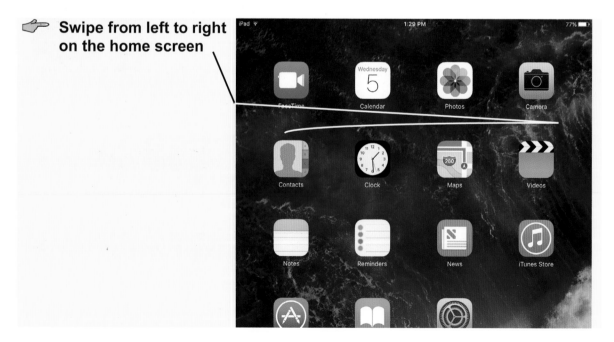

You see a previous installed app, for example *The Weather Channel*:

☞ **Press your finger on one of the apps**

The apps start vibrating, and an  appears in the top left corner. Now they can be moved around:

☞ **Drag** *Weather* **to the right, next to the other app**

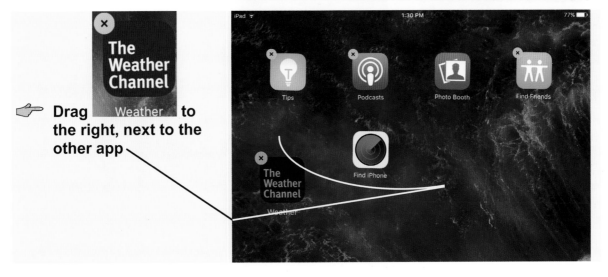

The apps have switched places. You can also move an app to a different page. You can put an app on the first page like this:

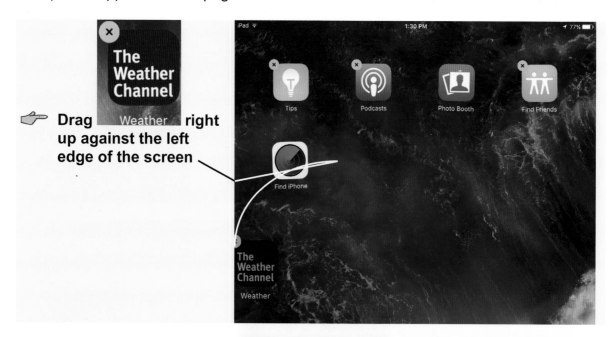

☞ **Drag** Weather **right up against the left edge of the screen**

As soon as you see the first screen:

☞ **Release** Weather

The app is now placed between the apps on the first screen:

On this page you can also rearrange the order of the apps to your liking. You do not need to do that now.

 **Press the Home button**

You can also store related apps in a folder. You do this as follows:

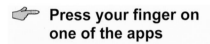 **Press your finger on one of the apps**

Drag the app on top of another app

A name is suggested for the folder:

If necessary, you can type another name:

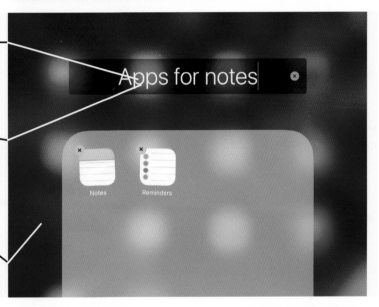

Tap the name

Type the desired name

If you are satisfied with the name:

Tap next to the folder

You see the new folder:

You can stop the apps from vibrating by pressing the Home button:

 **Press the Home button**

The apps are now static again. Now you can look at the contents of the new folder:

☞ **Tap** Apps for notes

You see the two apps that are in the folder:

If you want to remove an app from the folder:

☞ **Press your finger on one of the apps**

☞ **Drag the app outside the folder** ——

The app is now on the home screen again: ——

If you remove the other app from the folder as well, the folder will disappear.

☞ **Drag the other app outside the folder**

You can stop the apps from vibrating again:

 Press the Home button

3.14 Using Siri

Siri is the voice assistant for iPads and iPhones. You can ask *Siri* a question, but before doing so, you need to enable *Siri* in your *Settings*:

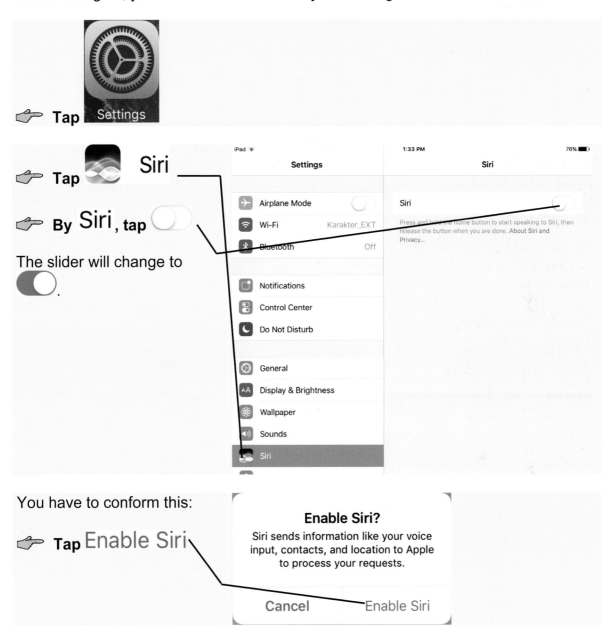

☞ **Tap** Settings

☞ **Tap** Siri

☞ **By** Siri **, tap** ⬭

The slider will change to ⬭.

You have to conform this:

☞ **Tap** Enable Siri

Enable Siri?

Siri sends information like your voice input, contacts, and location to Apple to process your requests.

Cancel   Enable Siri

You see additional settings for *Siri*:

By default, *Siri* speaks English and will have an American English voice. If necessary, you can also install a British English voice:

Siri always gives spoken feedback. If you only want spoken feedback when you use your iPad or iPhone hands-free, you can change the setting here:

By My Info , you select your own contact details, so *Siri* knows where you live, for example:

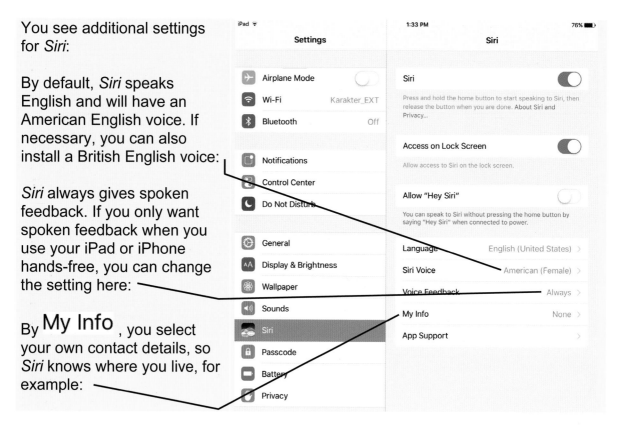

💡 **Tip**

Using Siri hands-free
In the *Tips* at the end of this chapter you can read how to install *Hey, Siri*, enabling you to use *Siri* hands-free when your iPad or iPhone is connected to a wall socket.

👉 **Press the Home button** ◯

You can ask *Siri* all kinds of different questions. For example, play all music by the Rolling Stones, when is my next appointment, switch on Wi-Fi, set a timer for five minutes, give me directions for home, send a message to Janet, show all my photos taken in Barcelona or set an appointment in my calendar for my hairdresser on Thursday at three o'clock.

This is how you activate *Siri*:

👉 **Press and hold the Home button** **pressed in**

You will hear a sound signal and the screen goes black. You can ask your question.

☞ **Question:** `What's the weather for New York?`

Siri will answer your question.

If you want to ask another question:

☞ **Tap**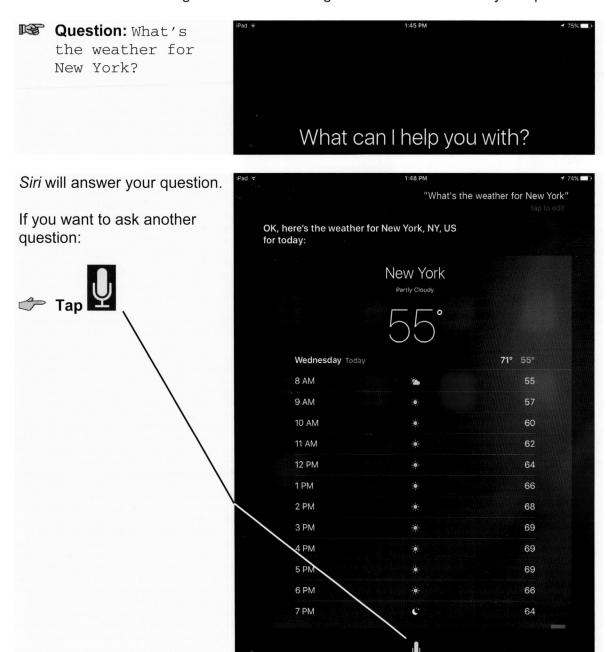

To return to the home screen:

☞ **Press the Home button**

3.15 Searching with Spotlight

Spotlight is the intelligent search system for the iPad and iPhone. It is a feature of the *Notification Center.* There are several ways to open *Spotlight*. From the home screen:

☞ **Swipe from the left edge to the right**

Spotlight is opened:

At the top you find a search field. This is the heart of *Spotlight*: ————

Siri app suggestions allows you to see your latest used contacts and apps: ————

Siri learns from your habits. If for example, you tend to read a book late at night, *Siri* will remember this and in the evening will display the *iBooks* app here:

 **Type in the search field:** `visual`

As soon as you start to type, various search results will appear: ——

If it is a long list, you can hide the keyboard to see more suggestions. On the keyboard:

 **Tap**

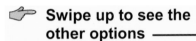 **Swipe up to see the other options** ——

If you would rather surf the Internet, or search in the *App Store* or the *Maps* app, you can use one of these links: ——

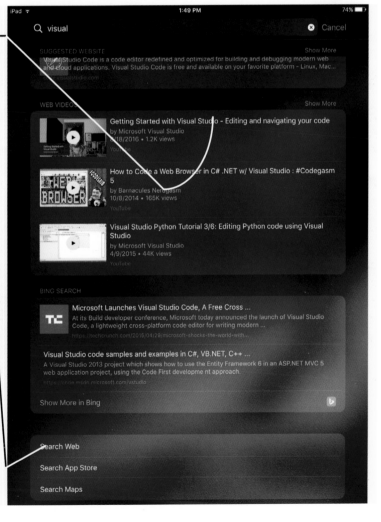

You can decide for yourself which apps *Spotlight* uses for a search:

☞ **Press the Home button**

☞ **Tap** Settings

☞ **If necessary, tap** General

☞ **Tap** Spotlight Search

By default, *Siri* suggestions are displayed, when you search with *Spotlight:*

Spotlight will search all apps and content in your iPad or iPhone:

If you do not want to see search results from the *App Store,* for example:

☞ **By** App Store, **tap**

The slider will now look like this .

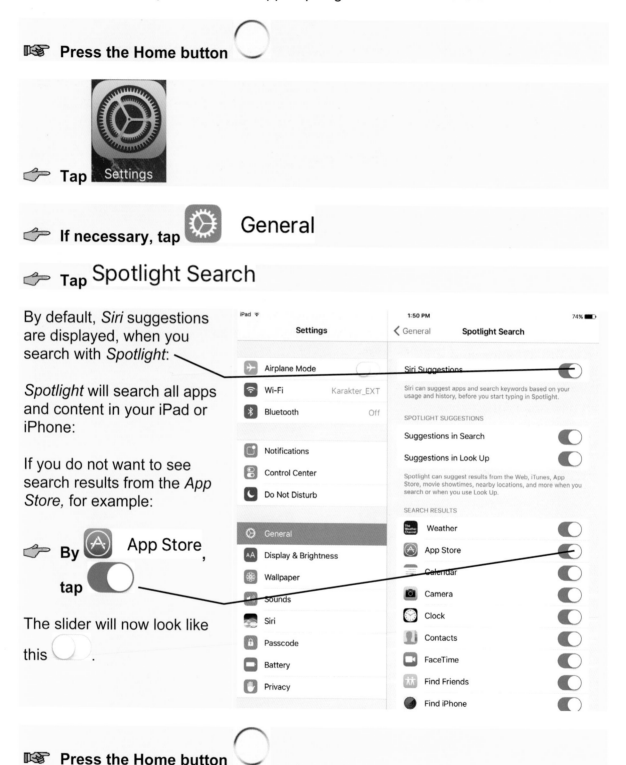

☞ **Press the Home button**

There is another quick way of opening *Spotlight*. This will work only if you have an app already opened.

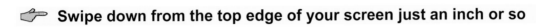 **Swipe down from the top edge of your screen just an inch or so**

Let go of the screen and you will see a transparent display of *Spotlight*. Here you can search on your iPad or iPhone and also on the Internet, the same way you use the regular version of *Spotlight*. To return to the app you were working with:

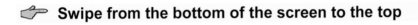 **Swipe from the bottom of the screen to the top**

3.16 iCloud

iCloud Drive is Apple's online storage service. In *iCloud Drive* you can save all kinds of files, even when they are not suitable for Apple software. These files can be synchronized with all of your devices that have enabled *iCloud Drive*. On all other devices you can look at and manage the files through the *iCloud* website www.icloud.com. *iCloud Drive* is usually enabled by default. You can check to see if this is the case for your own device:

Tap Settings

Tap iCloud , iCloud Drive

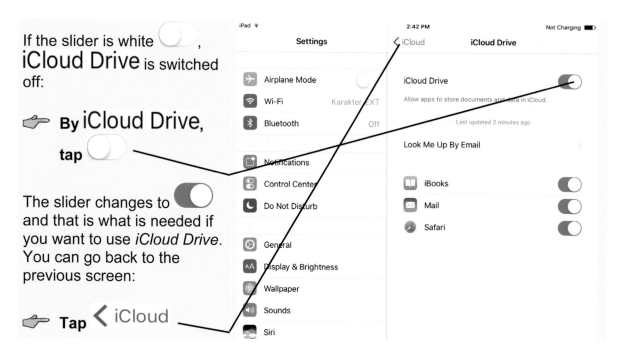

If the slider is white ⬭,
iCloud Drive is switched
off:

☞ By iCloud Drive,

tap ⬭

The slider changes to ⬤
and that is what is needed if
you want to use *iCloud Drive*.
You can go back to the
previous screen:

☞ Tap ‹ iCloud

By default, *iCloud* stores the data from *iBooks, Mail* and *Safari*, for example your favorite websites. On the iPad or iPhone, you can use the special *iCloud Drive* app to look at the files that are stored on *iCloud Drive*. This app is not one of the default apps, but it can be downloaded in the *App Store*. You can read how to download an app in *section 3.10 Downloading and Installing Apps*. This book does not elaborate any further on *iCloud*.

In this chapter you learned how to work with a variety of standard apps and features on the iPad or iPhone.

3.17 Tips

 Tip

Setting up Hey, Siri

Hey, Siri is a feature that automatically activates *Siri* when you say *Hey, Siri*. *Siri* must recognize your voice for this. This is how you set up *Hey, Siri*:

 Tap Settings , Siri

 By Allow "Hey Siri" , **tap**

 Tap Set Up Now

Siri will ask you to say a few sentences, ensuring that your voice will be recognized from now on:

🖝 **Speak out loud the sentences *Siri* displays**	Say "Hey Siri" into the iPad
If *Siri* does not understand you well: 🖝 **Try again**	Siri didn't quite get that. Try again.
Once *Siri* has understood all sentences correctly, you will see this notification: 🖝 **Tap** Done	"Hey Siri" Is Ready Siri will recognize your voice when your iPad is connected to power and you say, "Hey Siri." Done

Hey, Siri is now installed. *Siri* is activated on your iPad or iPhone as soon as you say *Hey, Siri*. The notification tells you to connect your device to a power source. But this is not correct; *Siri* also works even when the battery on your device is not charging.

🖝 **Press the Home button**

Tip

Using your Health app as a step counter/pedometer
The *Health* app can track all kinds of health functions. In most cases you need additional accessories for this. The step counter works without additional tools. Based on GPS data this app keeps track of how many steps you are taking daily. The app is only available for the iPhone.

☞ **Tap** Health

The first time you use the app you are asked to fill in your personal details, but this is not obligatory:

☞ **Tap** Next, Continue, Not Now, Not Now, Get Started

You will reach the main page, with different components:

☞ **Tap** Activity

- Continue on the next page -

By 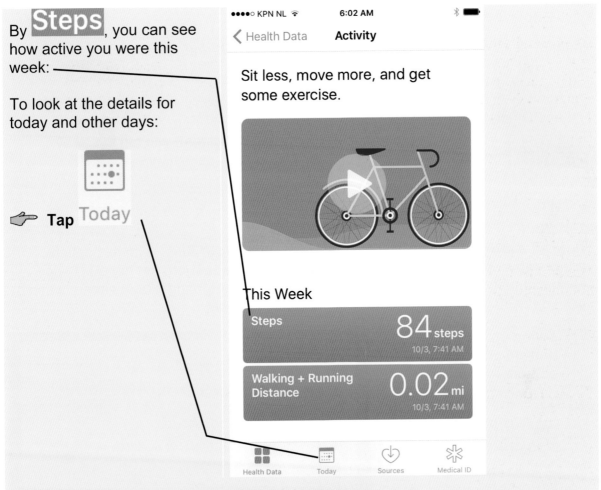 Steps, you can see how active you were this week:

To look at the details for today and other days:

☞ **Tap** Today

Sit less, move more, and get some exercise.

This Week

Steps — 84 steps — 10/3, 7:41 AM

Walking + Running Distance — 0.02 mi — 10/3, 7:41 AM

So, with your iPhone in your pocket you always have a step counter at hand. The phone does not need to be unlocked to keep track of your steps. However, the phone must be switched on, of course.

 Tip

Using the new Bedtime feature

The *Clock* app has a new feature: *Bedtime*. You can set the desired bedtime and wake-up times by answering a few questions. The iPad or iPhone will then set off an alarm to wake you up and will also alert you when it is time to go to sleep.

☞ **Tap** Clock , Bedtime

- Continue on the next page -

☞ **Follow the questions on your screen**

You now see information about your sleeping behavior, and you are advised to monitor your sleep history to ensure that you get enough sleep. Tap **Save** to store the information.

Bedtime is now turned on. To turn it off at any given moment, you tap ⬤⬜ by **Bedtime**.

💡 **Tip**
Night Shift
The iPad and iPhone contains another new feature: *Night Shift*. With this option, your screen becomes more yellow in color and is muted. There are several usage options: turning on Night Shift automatically at night, or turning it on by hand, when it suits you best. To turn on or disable Night Shift manually:

☞ **Swipe up from the bottom edge of your screen**

☞ **Tap**

☀🌙 **Night Shift: Off**

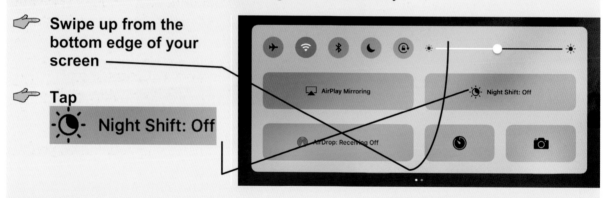

Night Shift will remain active till 7.00 AM if you choose Turn On Until 7 AM. Would you like to set up a schedule for Night Shift, allowing it to turn on and off automatically at certain times?

☞ Tap Schedule Settings...

☞ By Scheduled, tap ⬜

The slider will change to: ⬤. Night Shift will now turn on every night at 22.00 PM. and remain active till 7.00 AM the next morning. The night and morning time can be 10:00 PM

changed by tapping 7:00 AM and adjusting the times in the menu.

4. Photos and Video

The iPad and iPhone have both a front and a back camera. The camera feature is surely one of the main reasons that make these devices so popular. You can take pictures wherever you are and view them in the *Photos* app. The revamped *Photos* app in *iOS 10* features new *smart* folders. It automatically creates a folder for people and places.

Photos that you have taken on your device are collected together in the album called *Camera Roll*. Here you can create new folders and arrange your photos as desired. It is also possible to display photos on a map. When you view the map, it helps you refresh your memories about the destinations you have travelled to.

iOS 10 offers many new features for editing photos on the iPad and iPhone. You can annotate photos by adding a drawing, inserting text blocks and using a magnifier to highlight certain areas within a photo.

Smarter technology has also enhanced the ability to identify the content in your photos which makes it a lot easier to search through them. And if you start adding keywords, or names to your photos, it can be even faster.

When you record a video with the camera app, it is now possible to zoom in as you shoot. You can view your videos in the *Photo* app.

In this chapter you learn how to:

- take pictures with your iPad and iPhone;
- view pictures;
- create albums;
- sorting pictures into albums;
- viewing pictures on a map;
- edit and markup photos;
- draw on photos;
- do smart searches;
- record and play videos.

4.1 Taking Pictures

You can use the *Camera* app for taking photographs. In this section you practice with the camera on the back of your iPad or iPhone. The back camera is switched on by default when you launch the *Camera* app:

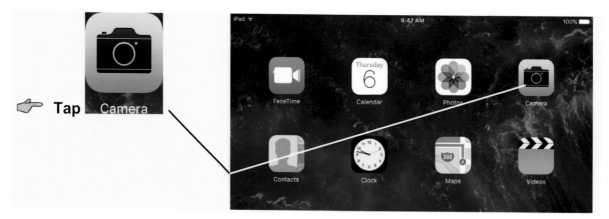

☞ **Tap** Camera

When you open the app for the first time you will be asked whether your current location can be used. This information is used to indicate where the photo was taken. In this example, it is allowed:

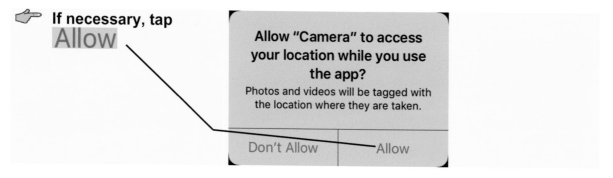

☞ **If necessary, tap** Allow

Right away you will see an image that can be taken with the camera on the back.

☞ **Direct the camera to an object you want to photograph**

Although the camera on the iPad and iPhone automatically focuses, you can choose to do this manually. You can shift the focus to a specific area within view:

☞ **Tap the desired area**

You see the picture is blurred for a short moment as the camera refocuses:

Next, the exposure is adjusted to the selected area. If you tap on a darker area of the object, you see that the image becomes brighter.
If the image becomes too bright, you can tap a lighter portion of the image.

Now you take the picture:

☞ **Tap**

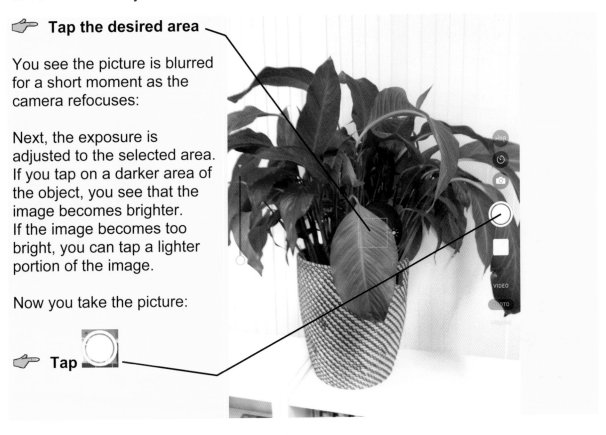

On the iPhone the shutter button looks just a little different:

You can take the picture:

☞ **Tap**

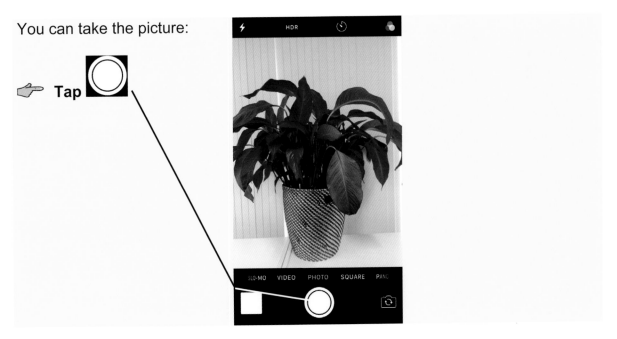

☞ **Take a couple more photos**

☞ **Press the Home button**

💡 **Tip**

Making square or panoramic photos
You can also make square or panoramic photos:

☞ Drag **SQUARE** or **PANO** to the center

On your iPhone you see these options above the white button.

With the **SQUARE** option, you will see a square area. You can take a picture in the same way as described above. With the **PANO** option, you will see a yellow guide and arrow. You turn or pan with your device over the area you want to shoot, keeping the point of the arrow on the line as you move. Instructions also appear on the screen.

💡 **Tip**

Zooming in
By using the digital zoom, you can zoom in on an object. This is only possible with the camera on the back of the iPhone. This is how you zoom in:

☞ **Spread your thumb and index finger away from each other on the screen**

To zoom out, you move your thumb and index finger towards each other.

💡 **Tip**

Unlocking the camera quickly
There is now a very fast way to launch the *Camera* app. On the lock screen, swipe you finger from right to left and the app will open.

4.2 Viewing Pictures

You can use the *Photos* app to view the pictures you have taken:

Tap Photos

You will see a screen where the photos are sorted by date, called *Collections*.

At the bottom of the screen:

Tap Albums

In the *Albums* display, the photos are sorted in folders:

Tap Camera Roll

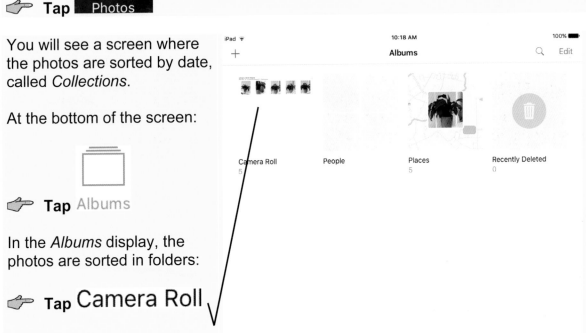

You see the miniatures of the photos and videos you have made:

Tap the first photo

The photo is enlarged. On the iPhone you see the same buttons as on the iPad, but they are at the bottom of the screen. On the iPad they are at the top. To browse to the next photo:

☞ **Drag from right to left over the photo**

To return to the previous photo, you drag from left to right.

On the iPad:

☞ Tap ❮ Camera Roll , ❮ Albums

On the iPhone:

☞ Tap ❮ , ❮ Albums

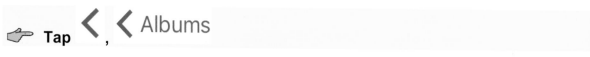

💡 **Tip**
Deleting a photo
You can delete a photo very simply:

☞ **If necessary, tap the photo**

☞ **Tap** 🗑

☞ **Tap** Delete Photo

Tip

Recently deleted?
The pictures you delete, are not actually 'gone'. They first appear in the folder *Recently Deleted*. You can delete them from there manually, if desired. If not, they are automatically deleted after 30 days, once they have been placed in this folder.

4.3 Creating New Albums

The *Photos* app has several standard albums, the *Camera Roll*, *People*, *Places*, *Screenshots* and *Recently Deleted*. Smart technology determines where the photos are placed. If you have not taken any screen shots, for example, the *Screenshots* album remains hidden. You can add additional folders to help you sort your photos more accurately.

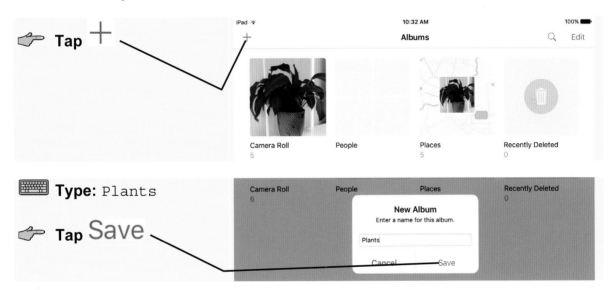

You can now add new photos directly to this new album:

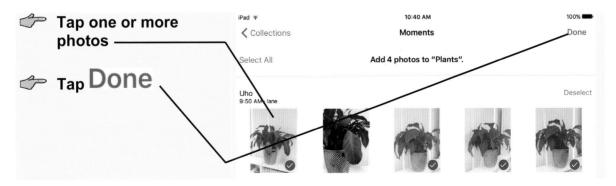

You can return to the *Albums* main page.

4.4 Sorting Pictures into Albums

All the pictures you take with your device can be found in the folder called *Camera Roll*. In addition, they can be sorted into one of the standard folders (*People*, *Places*) and the folders you created yourself.

☞ **Tap** Camera Roll

☞ **Tap** Select

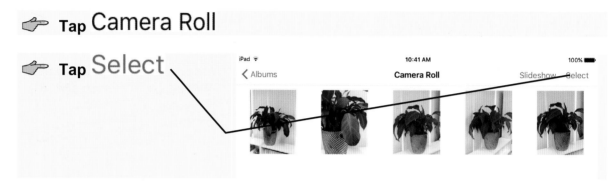

☞ **Tap the photo you want to copy to a certain folder**

On the iPad:

☞ **Tap** Add To

On the iPhone:

☞ **Tap** Add To

☞ **Tap** Plants

The photo is copied. It still remains in the *Camera Roll* folder but can now also be found in the *Plants* album.

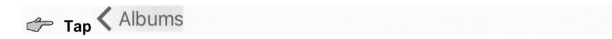

4.5 Viewing Pictures on a Map

In the *Photos* app you also see the album *Places,* where photos are sorted to, based on the location where they were taken. In addition, the app attempts to determine the location of the photo by its subject:

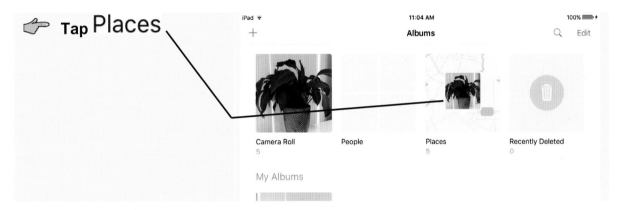

You see a country map. Some of the pictures you have taken are now displayed on this map. On your device, the map will look the same, but there will probably be other photos displayed from other places. You can zoom in with your fingers on the screen:

To zoom out, move your thumb and index finger towards each other.

You see an overview of all the pictures you have taken at that location:

 Tap a photo

If you only have one photo from that particular location that is all you will see. To return to the overview:

Again you see the country map. You can tap other locations to see whether photos have been made there.

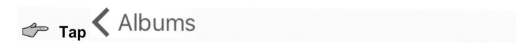

 Please note:
Only if your device was connected to the Internet as you took the photo, it will know where the photo was taken.

4.6 Editing Photos

A photo can sometimes be too dark or too light or have other shortcomings. The *Photos* app has a number of options that can help to improve this. With Auto-enhance a 'bad' photo can look a whole lot better right away. This feature automatically adjusts the exposure and saturation of a photo:

 Tap the desired album

 Tap the photo you want to edit

 Please note:
In this section and the following ones, some practice photos are used that were copied to the iPad or iPhone. To perform these steps, you can use your own photos, make some new photos or just read through the sections without practicing.

Tap ⚙

On the iPhone, you see this button at the bottom of your screen.

To automatically enhance the photo:

Tap 🪄

On the iPhone, this button is at the top. The photo is enhanced:

Tap 🪄 again and you see the original photo as it was.

Tap 🎛 to adjust the light and color settings:

Tap ⬤ to add a filter:

To save the edited photo:

Tap

🖐 Please note:

The original photo will be replaced by the edited photo.

To return to the photo album:

☞ **Tap the name of the album or**

❮ Camera Roll

(iPad) or ❮ (iPhone)

4.7 Drawing on Photos

New in *iOS 10* is the option to draw on your photos, or in other words, add markup or tags. This can be useful as a reminder to yourself, for example, by adding someone's name to a photo made at a party, or adding a note or comment to a really nice photo.

☞ **Tap the desired album**

☞ **Tap the photo you want to draw on**

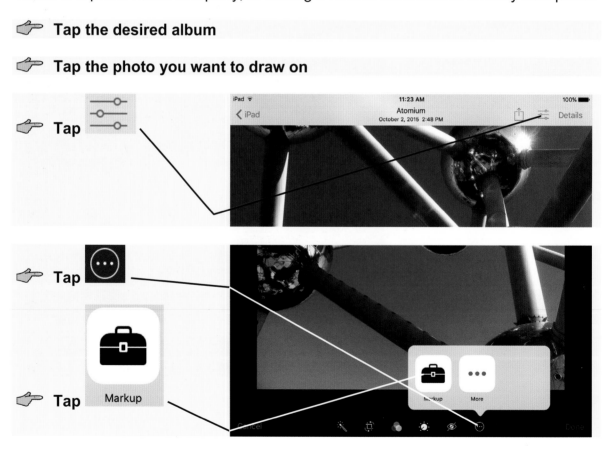

☞ **Tap**

☞ **Tap**

☞ **Tap** Markup

In the *Markup* window there are several options for drawing and adding tags to your photos. You activate this feature by tapping it. Then you can start to work on the photograph. The images in this section are made on the iPad. The iPhone works the same, only the buttons are in a different place. You can use this feature like this:

☞ **Move your finger over the screen to draw or write something**

You can always undo your actions if you are not satisfied with the effect:

☞ **Tap** 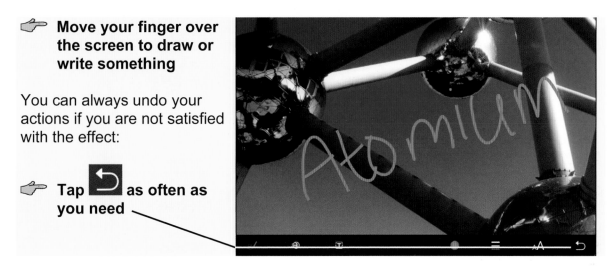 **as often as you need**

You can also enlarge a part of the picture to accent that area:

☞ **Tap**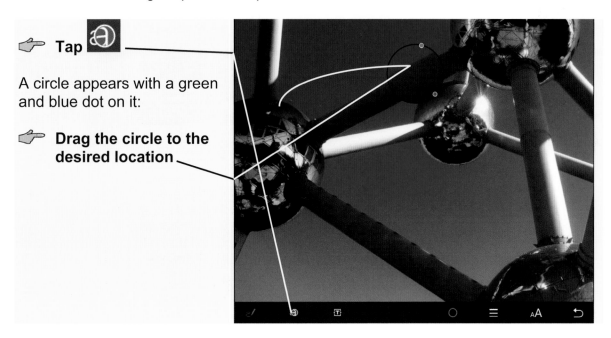

A circle appears with a green and blue dot on it:

☞ **Drag the circle to the desired location**

You can increase or decrease the circle:

☞ **Drag the blue dot outwards** —

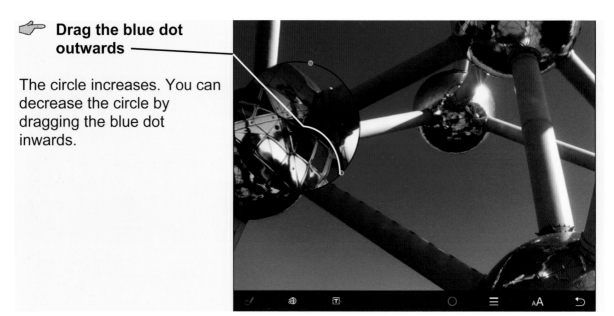

The circle increases. You can decrease the circle by dragging the blue dot inwards.

You can set the zooming degree with the green dot:

☞ **Drag the green dot over the edge of the circle** —

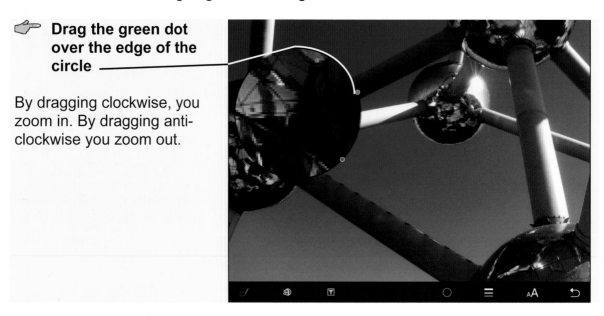

By dragging clockwise, you zoom in. By dragging anti-clockwise you zoom out.

Are you satisfied with the content inside the circle?

☞ **Tap outside the circle**

You can also add a text block to the photo, for example, to add a comment or note:

☞ **Tap**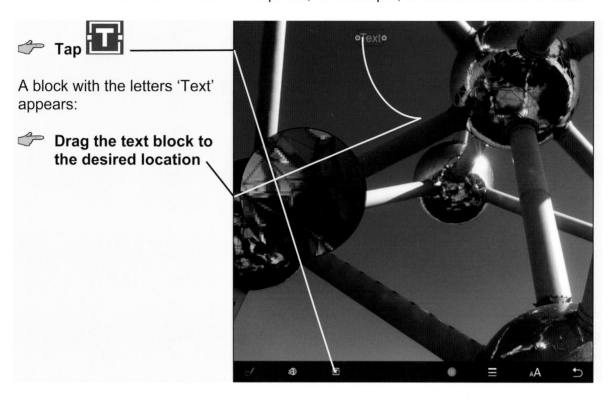

A block with the letters 'Text' appears:

☞ **Drag the text block to the desired location**

The blue dots will help you adjust the width of the text block:

☞ **Drag the left blue dot to the left**

The block is now wider. You can decrease the width of the block on the left in the same manner. To widen or decrease the right side, use the blue dot on the right.

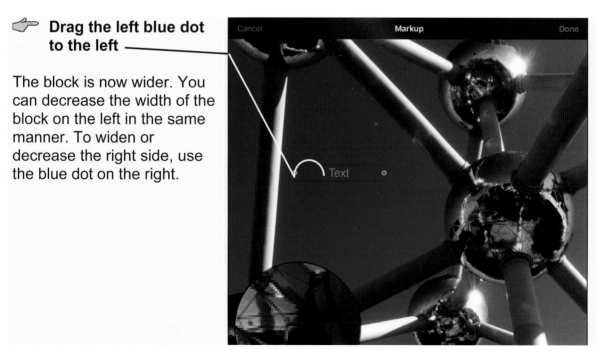

Now you can type one or more words in the text field.

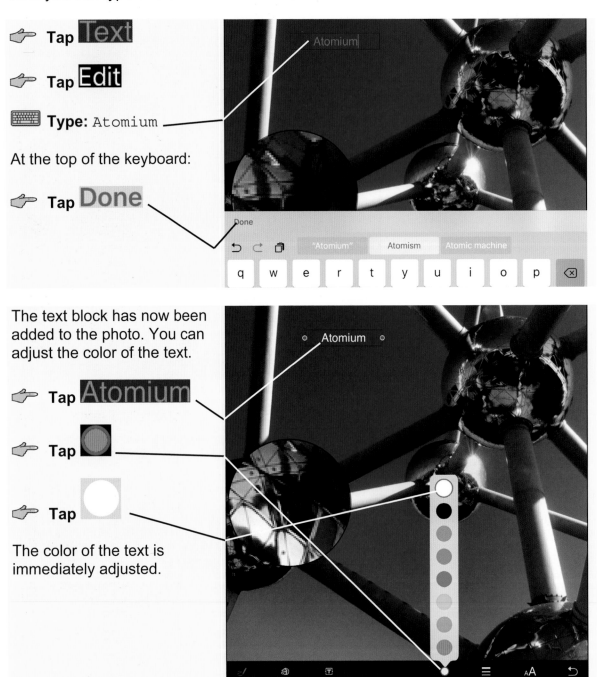

☞ **Tap** Text

☞ **Tap** Edit

⌨ **Type:** Atomium

At the top of the keyboard:

☞ **Tap** Done

The text block has now been
added to the photo. You can
adjust the color of the text.

☞ **Tap** Atomium

☞ **Tap** 🔘

☞ **Tap** ⚪

The color of the text is
immediately adjusted.

There is an outline around the text block. You can adjust the thickness of the outline easily. This option is only available on the iPad:

👉 **Tap** Atomium

👉 **Tap** ☰

👉 **Tap** ⊙

The thickness of the outline is immediately adjusted.

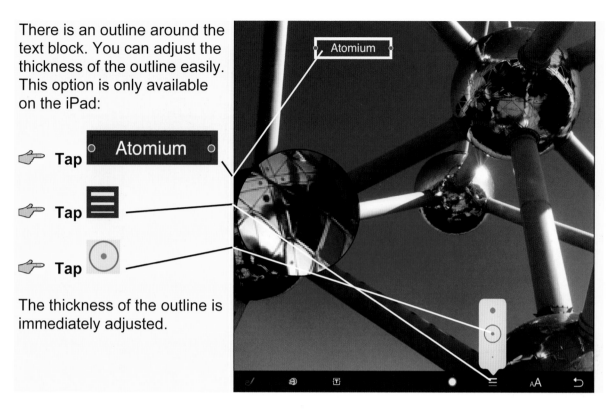

Also the font can be adjusted. This can be done on the iPhone, too.

👉 **Tap** Atomium

👉 **Tap** AA

You see a list with different fonts:

👉 **Tap the desired font**

To increase or decrease the letters:

👉 **Drag the slider**

👉 **Tap outside the text**

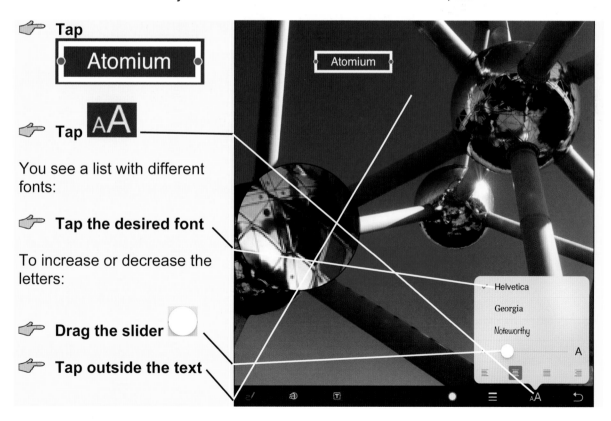

Have you finished editing the photo? You can save the changes and return to the photo in the overview:

☞ **Tap** Done, Done

If you do not want to save the changes, you can return to the original photo in the overview:

☞ **Tap** Cancel, Cancel, Discard Changes

4.8 Smart Photo Search

Smart technology makes searching through photos in *iOS 10* a lot easier. Each photo you take is analyzed extensively. The system actively tries to recognize what you photographed. All the data is linked together, making your photographs easier to find.

☞ **Tap** Photos

You will see several folders along with the search icon. In this search box, you can type words that are related to the photo, including the place where the photo was taken:

☞ **Tap** 🔍

⌨ **Type:** Atomium

As you are typing, some results appear:

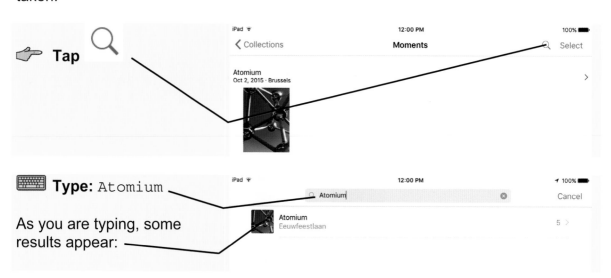

As you create more photos, this feature works better. By tapping the photo, you enlarge it. At the top, tap left of the name of the folder to return to the search results.

 **Tap** ‹ Search

Have you finished searching?

 **Tap** Cancel

 Press the Home button

Tip
Memories
The *Memories* feature is new in *iOS 10* as well. *Memories* are albums that are automatically created and linked to an event. Think of the photos you created during a weekend or holiday. *Memories* are put together independently by *iOS 10*. You can view each of the photos in a memory separately, or through a video show with music in the background.

4.9 Recording and Playing Videos

You can use the camera of the iPad and iPhone for recording video:

 Tap Camera

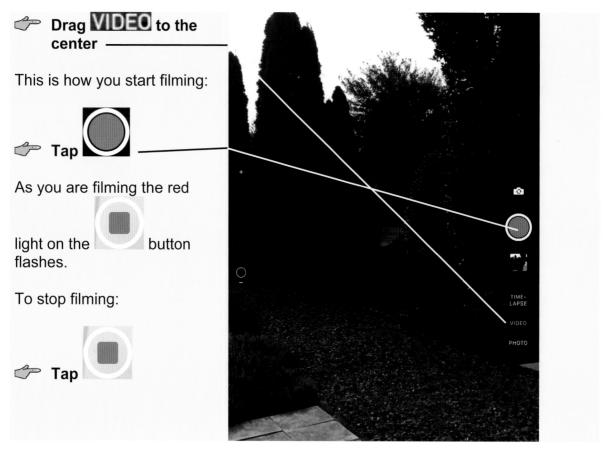

☞ **Drag** **VIDEO** **to the center** ─────────

This is how you start filming:

☞ **Tap**

As you are filming the red

light on the button flashes.

To stop filming:

☞ **Tap**

💡 **Tip**

Landscape
If you would like to play your videos back on a TV or computer screen, you should hold your device in landscape mode. This will give you a nice full screen image.

💡 **Tip**

Focusing
Before and during filming, you can focus on the object of your choice, the same way you do when taking pictures.

☞ **Tap the object you want to focus**

Here, the exposure is also adjusted to the selected object. If you tap on a dark part of the object, you see that the image lights up. If the image becomes too bright, touch a darker part of the object.

☞ **Press the Home button**

You can view your videos in the *Photos* app. You can watch a video you made earlier:

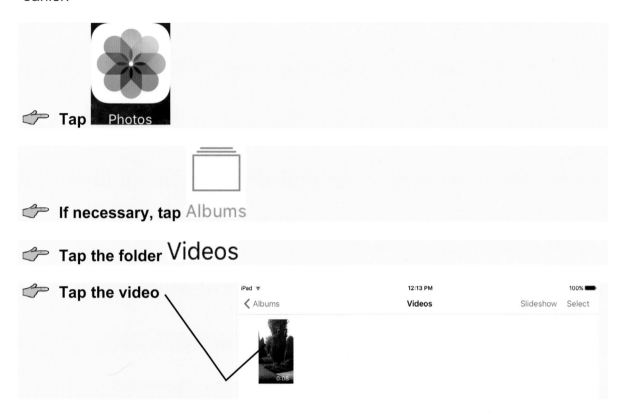

☞ **Tap** Photos

☞ **If necessary, tap** Albums

☞ **Tap the folder** Videos

☞ **Tap the video**

The video in this example is made in the upright (portrait) mode. If you have a video made in landscape mode, then rotate your device a quarter turn.

You see your video. To play the video:

☞ **Tap**

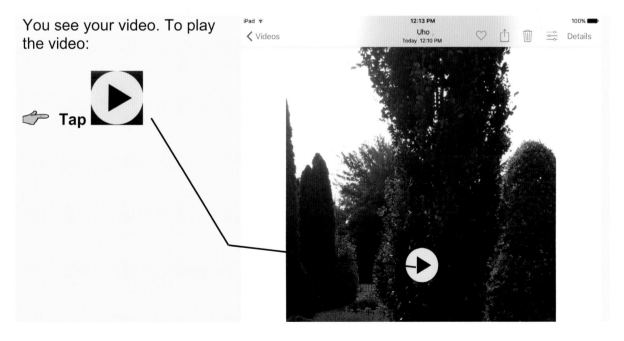

The video fills the screen:

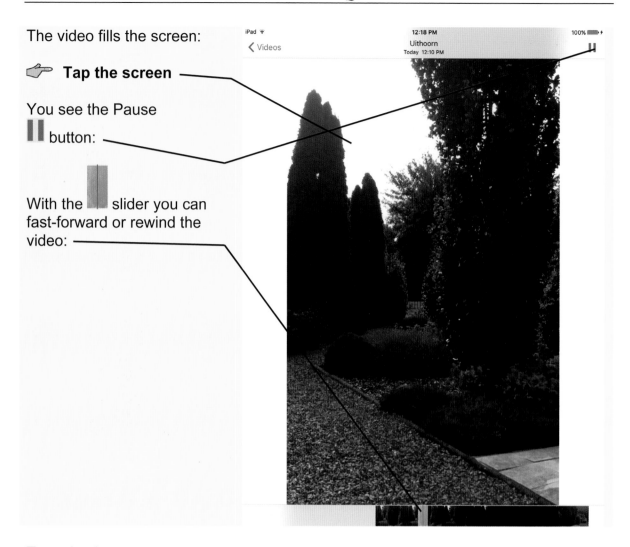

👉 **Tap the screen**

You see the Pause ▮▮ button:

With the ▮▮ slider you can fast-forward or rewind the video:

To go back:

👉 **Tap** ‹ Videos

👉 **Tap** ‹ Albums

👉 **Press the Home button** ◯

4.10 Tips

 Tip

Using the Photos app in several other ways
The *Photos* app has a number of options that allows you to share photos, or use them in other ways:

 Open a photo

☞ **Tap** ⬆️

You can select a number of photos by tapping them:

A selection of the options:

Message: a new SMS or *iMessage* opens with the photo attached.

Facebook: if you have linked your *Facebook* account to your device, you can open a new message with (a link to) the photo.

Slideshow: you can play a slideshow with the selected photos.

Assign to Contact : the list with contacts is opened. You can select a photo to represent a particular contact. You can also increase or decrease the size of the photo.

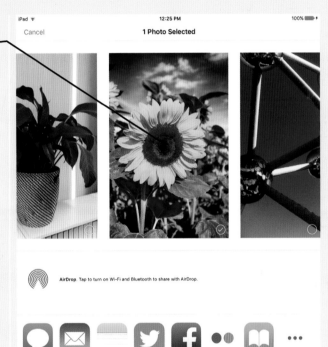

Use as Wallpaper: you use your photograph as background for your lock screen or home screen of your device.

Print: print a photo with a printer suitable for AirPrint.

You can find these options by dragging over the row of options from right to left.

Notes

Write your notes down here.

5. Music and Apple Music

On your iPad or iPhone, you can listen to the music you put on it yourself. The easiest way to do this is by using the *iTunes* program. You can listen to the songs with the *Music* app.

However, listening to online music is also an option. *Apple Music* is a streaming music service from Apple that lets you listen to unlimited music from a catalog of more than thirty million songs. *Streaming* means that the music is played over the Internet. *Apple Music* is comparable with the popular *Spotify* music service.

Apple Music was launched end of June 2015. To introduce as many people as possible to *Apple Music*, this service is offered for free for the first three months. During these three months you can listen to unlimited music. *Apple Music* adapts to your preferences and makes new suggestions based on the music you have played.

Apple Music does not have its own app; the service is part of the *Music* app. In this app you can also find various radio stations from *Apple Music* and Apple's own radio station *Beats One*. The station broadcasts live 24 hours a day, with DJs in London, Los Angeles and New York.

In this chapter you learn how to:

- add music from your PC to your iPad or iPhone;
- listen to songs with the *Music* app;
- activate *Apple Music* and choose your favorite genres and artists;
- listen to music with *Apple Music*;
- search for music;
- create and delete a playlist;
- cancel your subscription to *Apple Music*.

 Please note:

In this section you start by taking a look at the *Music* app in general. Later, you will learn how to listen to music with *Apple Music*. If you have activated this service, it will not be possible to transfer separate songs to your iPad or iPhone as well. This is probably done with the idea that all the music you might want, is already available with *Apple Music*, so you do not need additional individual songs anymore. If you decide later to add individual songs to your iPad or iPhone, you must first deactivate *Apple Music*. We explain how to do that in *section 5.8 Unsubscribe from Apple Music*.

5.1 Adding Music from the PC to your iPad or iPhone

Listen to your favorite CD on your iPhone or iPad. Once the tracks are in *iTunes*, they can easily be added to your iPad or iPhone. In this section it is assumed that *iTunes* is already installed on your computer. If that is not the case, you can install *iTunes* from the web www.apple.com/nl/itunes/download.

☞ **Connect your device to the computer**

☞ **Open *iTunes* on the computer**

⊕ **Click** Library

⊕ **Click** ♪ **Songs**

You see the music tracks in *iTunes*:

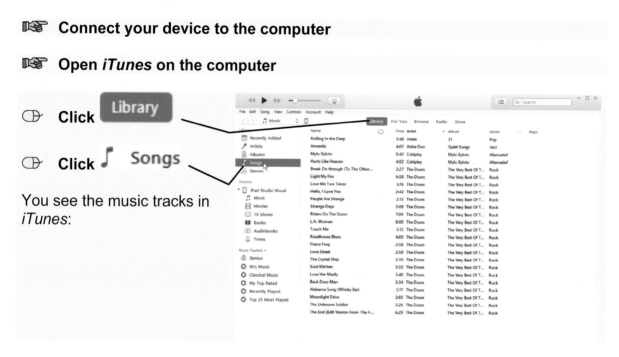

In *iTunes* you select the tracks you want to transfer:

⊕ **Click the first track**

⌨ **Press** Shift **and hold it down**

⊕ **Click the third track**

⌨ **Release** Shift

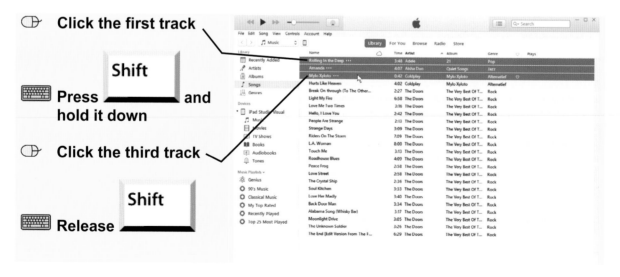

The tracks are selected. Now copy these songs to your device. Once you start dragging the tracks, on the left-hand side of the window the *Devices* section will appear showing the content of the connected iPad or iPhone:

☞ **Drag the selection to the left-hand side to**

   🔲 iPad Studio Visual

The pointer will change to
:

☞ **Release the mouse button**

The songs will be copied.

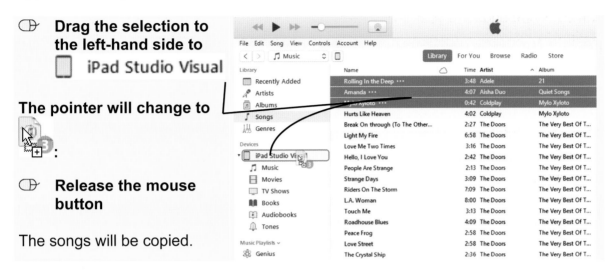

You can view the content on your device, in this case an iPad:

☞ **Click**

   🔲 iPad Studio Visual

☞ **Click 🎵 Music**

You see that the tracks have been added:

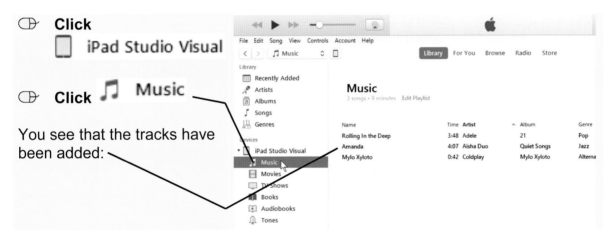

You can disconnect your iPad or iPhone:

☞ **Disconnect your iPad or iPhone from your computer safely**

☞ **Close *iTunes***

5.2 Playing Music with the Music App

This is the way to play a track on your iPad or iPhone:

☞ **Tap** Music

The first time you use the *Music* app, you will see a window about *Apple Music*, the music streaming service from Apple. You do not need to use this yet, but later on:

☞ **Tap** Not Now

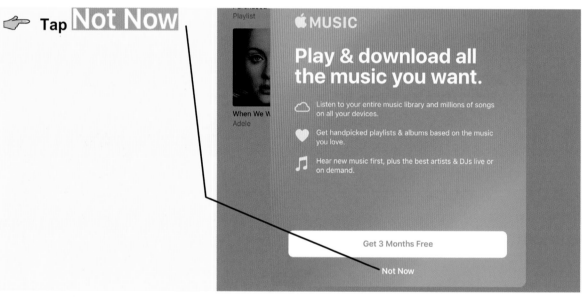

If necessary, at the bottom of the screen:

☞ **Tap** Library

Here you see an overview of the albums and tracks you stored on your device via *iTunes*.

☞ **Tap a folder of an artist or album**

Here you see the track that
was copied in the previous
section:

☞ **Tap the title**

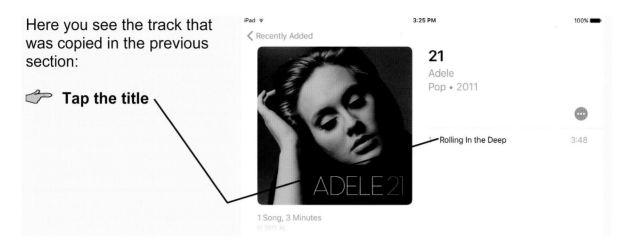

The track is played. At the bottom of the screen:

☞ **Tap the title of the
track**

You see several buttons that
allows you to control the
music:

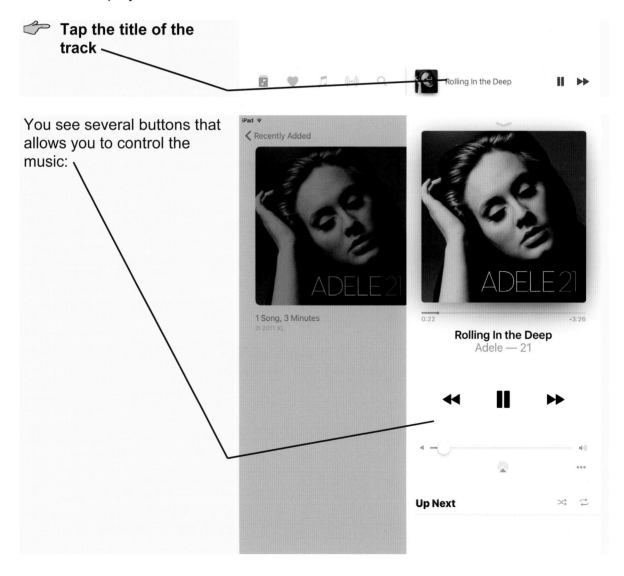

The buttons have the following functions:

0:09   Drag ⬤ in the scrubber bar to move to a different position in the song.

⏪   This button has multiple functions:
- tap once: go to the beginning of the current track.
- tap twice: go the previous track.
- tap and hold your finger on it: rewind.

⏩   This button has multiple functions:
- tap once: go to the next track.
- tap and hold your finger on it: fast-forward.

⏸   Play/Pause.

▶   Resume playback.

     Volume control.

🔀   Play in random order.

🔁   Repeat, you see the next options:

- 🔁 : do not use repeat.

- 🔁 : all tracks will be repeated.

- 🔁¹ : the current track is repeated.

•••   Opens a new menu with, among others, the options: add tracks to a playlist, or remove a track.

♥   This button you see after you tapped ••• . This option allows you to turn some tracks into your favorites. You will then get suggestions for other tracks you may like. To be able to use this option, you need have a subscription to *Apple Music*.

🚫♥   Remove a track from your list of favorites.

While playing your music, you can leave the *Music* app and do something else:

☞ **Press the Home button**

The music will continue playing in the background. From any app on your device, you can bring up the control buttons of the *Music* app like this:

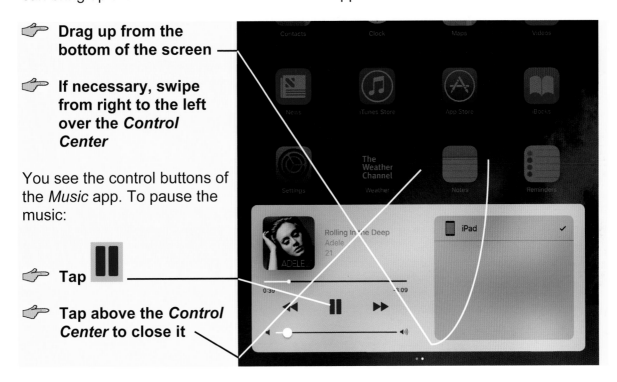

☞ **Drag up from the bottom of the screen** ——

☞ **If necessary, swipe from right to the left over the *Control Center***

You see the control buttons of the *Music* app. To pause the music:

☞ **Tap** ——————

☞ **Tap above the *Control Center* to close it** ⟍

You see the home screen.

5.3 Activating Apple Music

Apple Music is a music streaming service comparable to *Spotify*. You can take out a trial subscription for free and see if it is something for you. You can listen to unlimited music for three months. *Apple Music* does not have its own app. This service is part of the *Music* app.

 Please note:

In this and the next few sections you will be learning about *Apple Music*. If you activate this service, your own songs will remain in the *Library*, but it is not yet possible to manually add new songs to your device while using *Apple Music*.

 Please note:

In order to use the free trial, you have to subscribe to the service. If you decide not to use *Apple Music* anymore, you can unsubscribe before the three months have elapsed. In *section 5.8 Unsubscribe from Apple Music* you can read how to do this.

Please note:

To use the free trial period, you will be asked for your credit card details to be linked to your *Apple ID*. No money will be debited during the first three months.

You first set up *Apple Music*:

☞ **Tap** Music

☞ **Tap** ♥ For You

☞ **Tap** Choose Your P

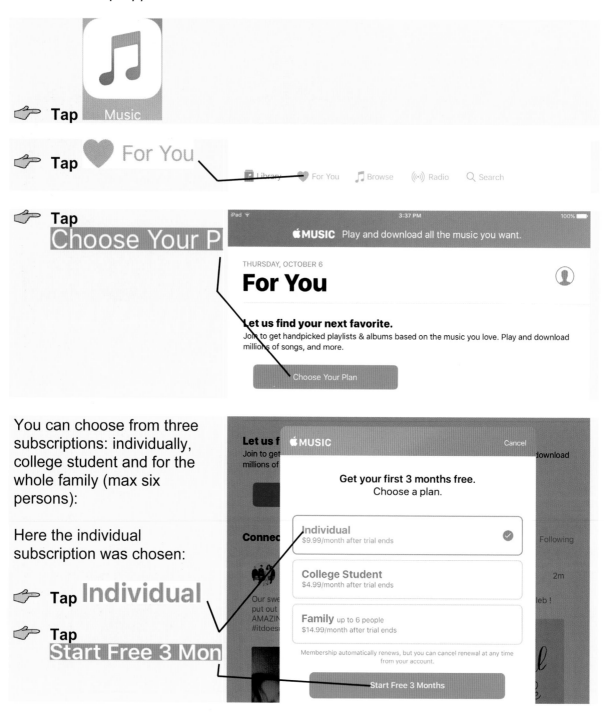

You can choose from three subscriptions: individually, college student and for the whole family (max six persons):

Here the individual subscription was chosen:

☞ **Tap** Individual

☞ **Tap** Start Free 3 Mon

To make use of the free trial period, your credit card credentials must be linked to your *Apple ID*. For the first three months no money will be debited from your account.

☞ **Follow the instructions on the screen to subscribe to *Apple Music***

For starters, *Apple Music* wants to know your taste in music. For this a special system has been developed. Pink circles appear with genres or names of artists. The circles that do not appeal to you will disappear with a firm press. Circles with names or genres that do appeal to you can be tapped to enlarge them:

☞ **Tap the circles of the genres you like** ——

The circles increase:

☞ **Tap twice on the circles with the genres you like best**

These circles increase even more:

☞ **Press and hold the circles of the genres you do not like, until they disappear**

When you are left with the desired genres:

☞ **Tap Next**

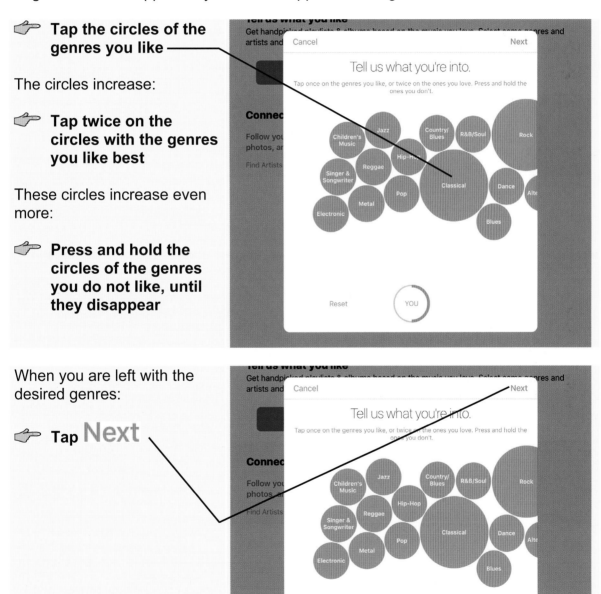

You do the same with the artists that are introduced by *Apple Music*:

☞ **Follow the same procedure with the introduced artists**

To see more artists:

☞ **Tap** More Artists

After you have chosen your favorite artists, at the top of the screen:

☞ **Tap** Done

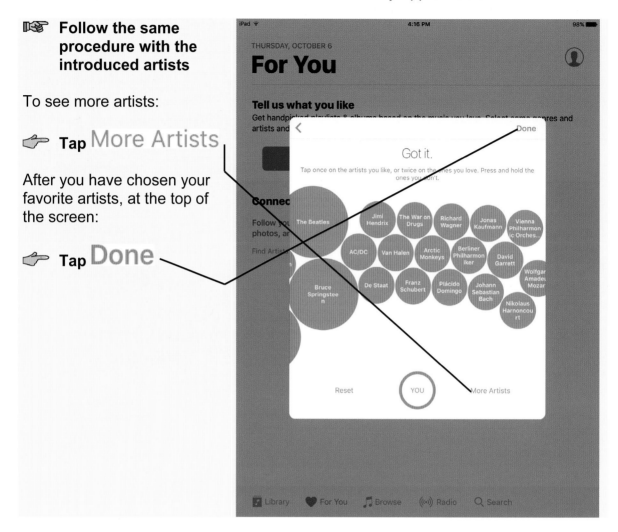

Apple Music now opens. It starts on the *Library* tab. There you can find all the music on your device. But the *Library* is not the only location where you can find music:

☞ **Tap** 🎵 Library

At the top you see a number of standard playlists in this example:

With 🔍 Search you can look specifically for artists, albums and songs:

With the tab 📻 Radio you can listen to online radio stations:

The tab 🎵 Browse will let you discover new music:

The tab 💜 For You collects the music *Apple Music* thinks you will appreciate:

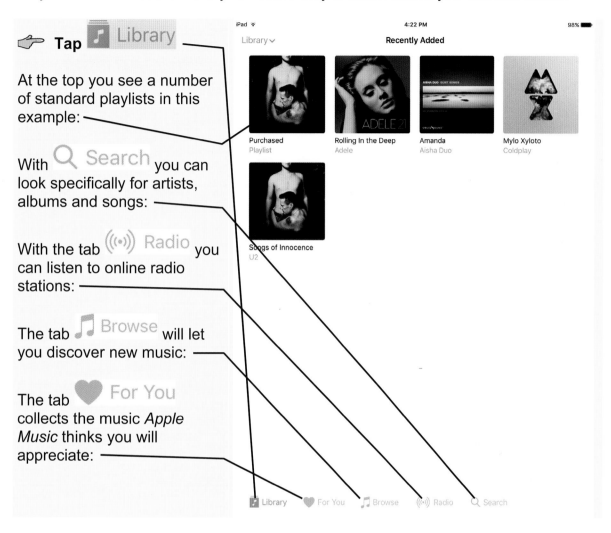

5.4 Listening to Music by Apple Music

On the tab 💜 For You you see suggestions for playlists and albums based on your given preferences. This is how you make a playlist:

☞ **Tap** 💜 For You

☞ **Tap a suggested playlist**

On your own screen you see of course other suggestions.

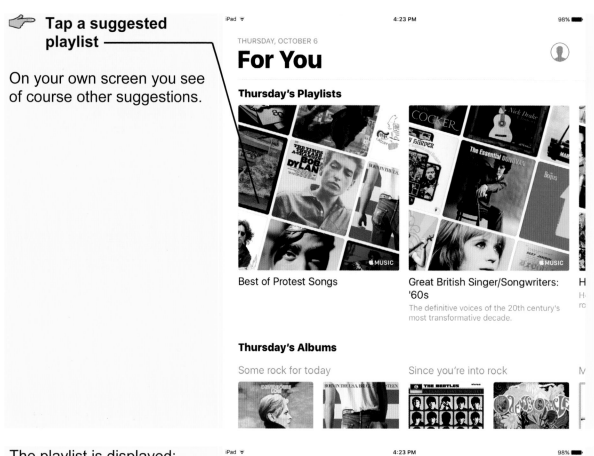

The playlist is displayed:

☞ **Tap the first track**

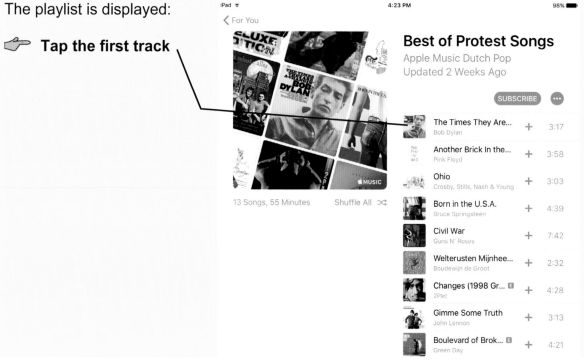

The song starts playing. You see a miniature of the album cover at the bottom. You can enlarge this:

☞ **Tap the picture of the album cover**

The song is played and the cover of the related album is displayed:

The buttons you see have the same functions as shown before: ──────

To return to the playlist:

☞ **Tap next to the play window**

This way you play the playlist in random order:

☞ **Tap** Shuffle All

Another song from the list is played.

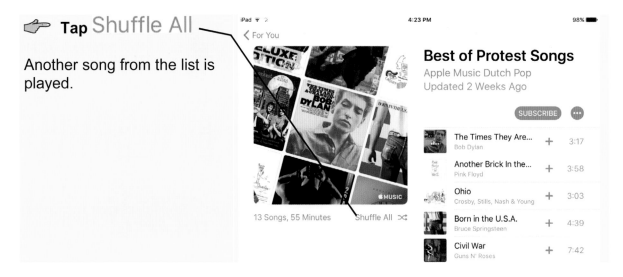

5.5 Searching for Music

If you want to search for music from a certain artist, you can use the search function. Try it out:

☞ **Tap** 🔍

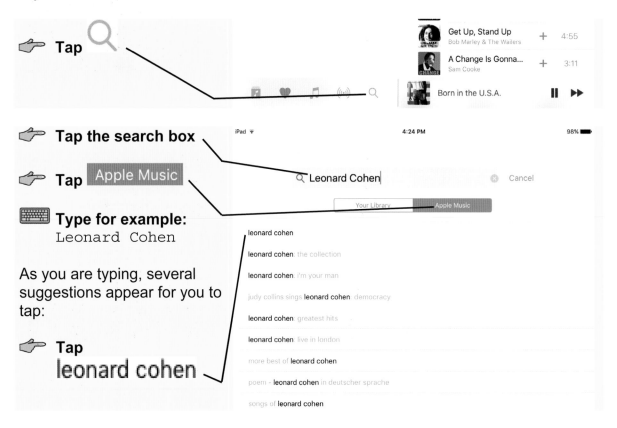

☞ **Tap the search box**

☞ **Tap** Apple Music

⌨ **Type for example:**
Leonard Cohen

As you are typing, several suggestions appear for you to tap:

☞ **Tap**
leonard cohen

👉 **Tap**

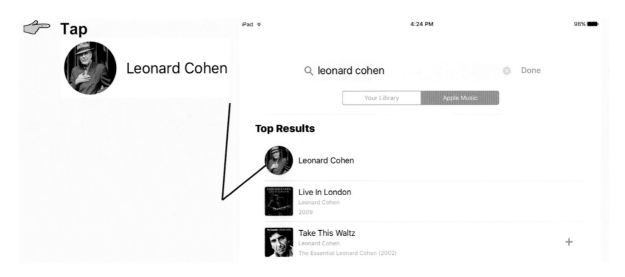

You see the artist page from Leonard Cohen:

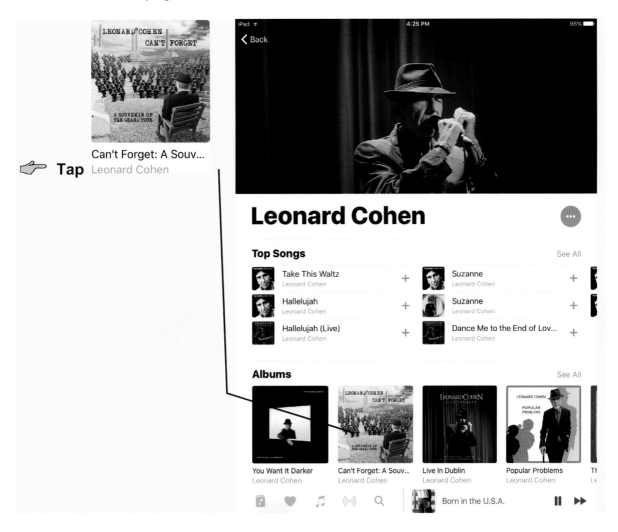

This album can be played in the same manner as the playlist in the last section.

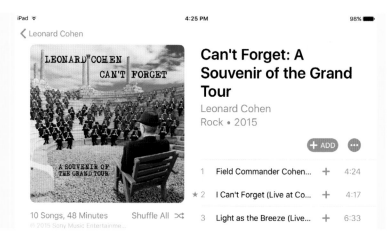

5.6 Creating a Playlist

In a playlist you can put together your favorite music. For example, you can make a playlist with music you like to hear while you read or cook. You do this as follows:

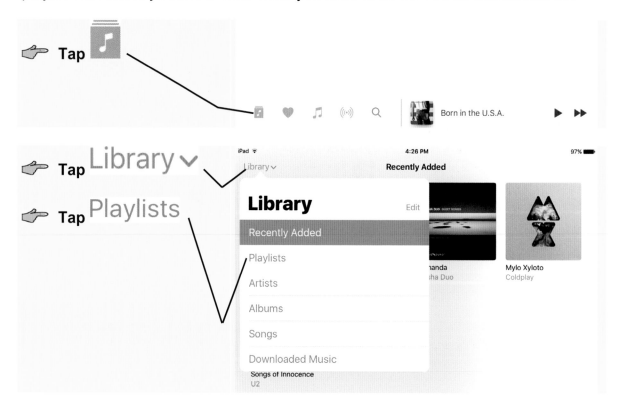

👉 **Tap** New

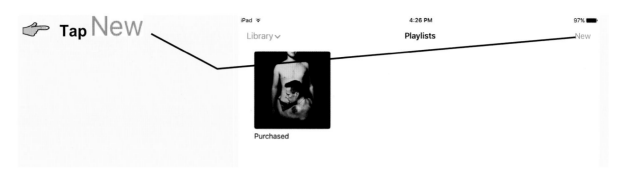

First you give the playlist a recognizable name:

👉 **Tap**
Playlist Name

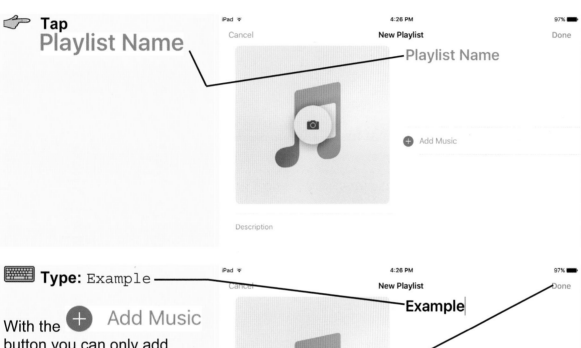

⌨️ **Type:** Example

With the ➕ Add Music button you can only add tracks you have stored on your iPad or iPhone. To add music from *Apple Music*:

👉 **Tap** Done

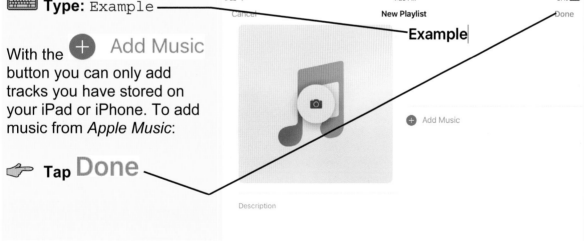

At the bottom of the screen:

👉 **Tap**

Again you see the playlist of *Apple Music*. You can add an album to your new playlist as follows:

☞ **By the desired album,**

 tap

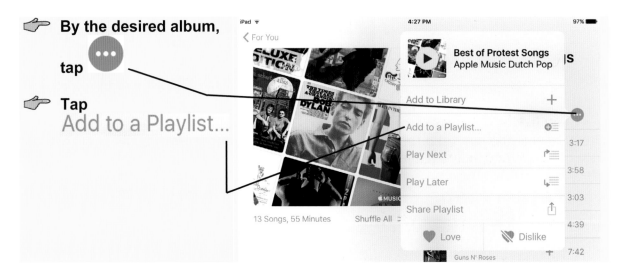

☞ **Tap**

You may see the notification that the *iCloud* music library is required for adding music to *My music.* In that case:

You choose the new playlist:

Example

☞ **Tap**

The tracks are added to the playlist.

 Tip

Adding other music
You can add all music from the *Music* app to your playlist. Not just the music you can find via the search field, but also the music that is already stored on your iPad or iPhone.

To play the playlist:

☞ **Tap**

☞ **Tap** Example

☞ **Tap the first song**

The playlist is now being played.

5.7 Removing the Playlist

A playlist you no longer use, can be removed like this:

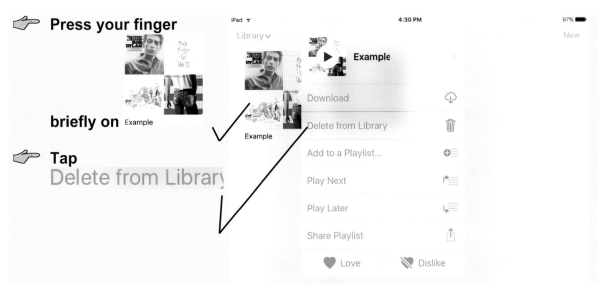

☞ **Press your finger**

briefly on Example

☞ **Tap**
Delete from Library

☞ **Tap**
Delete Playlist

The playlist is removed.

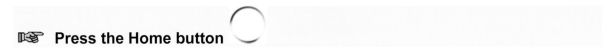

☞ **Press the Home button**

5.8 Unsubscribing from Apple Music

If you do not want to you use *Apple Music* anymore once your free trial period is over, you can cancel your subscription as follows. Be sure to do this before the three months has elapsed:

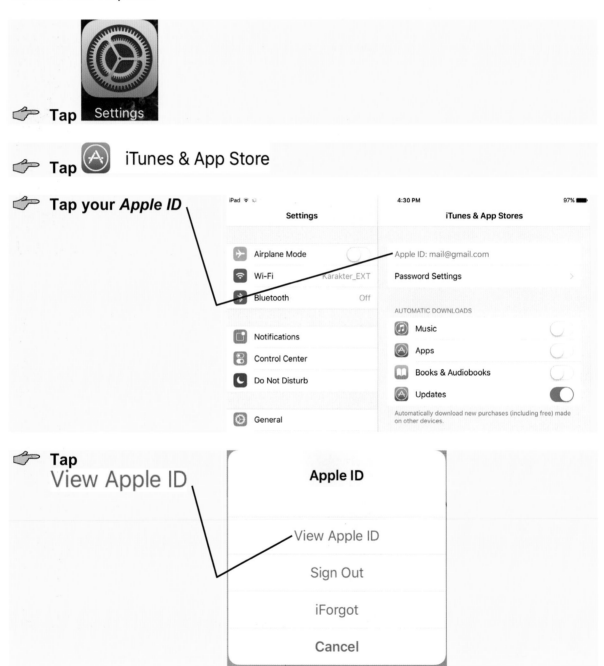

👉 **Tap** Settings

👉 **Tap** (A) iTunes & App Store

👉 **Tap your** *Apple ID*

👉 **Tap**
   View Apple ID

You look for your subscriptions:

☞ **By**
SUBSCRIPTIONS
tap Manage

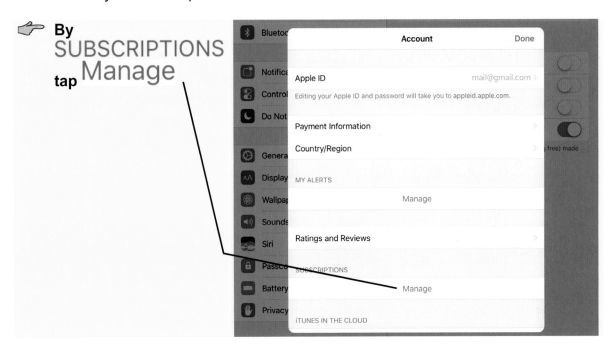

You see the details of your *Apple Music* subscription:

You can cancel the
subscription. It will still
continue for the remainder of
the three months, but will
then stop automatically:

☞ **Tap**
Cancel Subscription

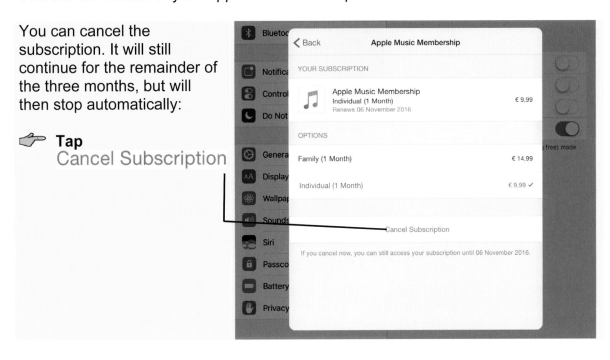

This you have to confirm:

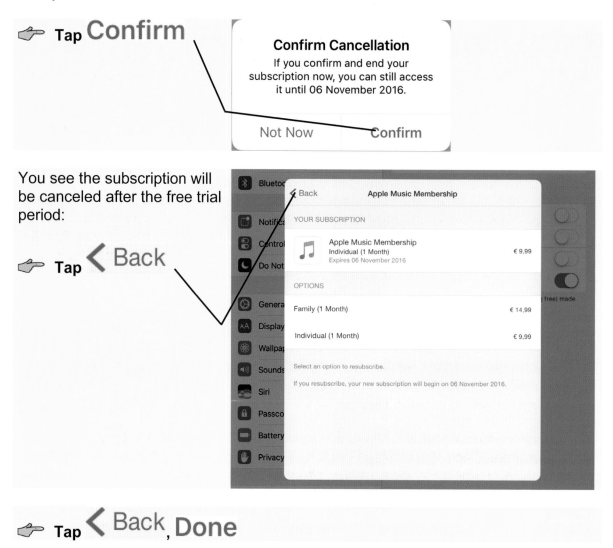

☞ **Tap** Confirm

Confirm Cancellation
If you confirm and end your subscription now, you can still access it until 06 November 2016.

Not Now   Confirm

You see the subscription will be canceled after the free trial period:

☞ **Tap** ❮ Back

Back   Apple Music Membership

YOUR SUBSCRIPTION

Apple Music Membership
Individual (1 Month)   € 9,99
Expires 06 November 2016

OPTIONS

Family (1 Month)   € 14,99

Individual (1 Month)   € 9,99

Select an option to resubscribe.

If you resubscribe, your new subscription will begin on 06 November 2016.

☞ **Tap** ❮ Back, **Done**

Your subscription to *Apple Music* will end after the free trial period.

☞ **Press the Home button**

In this book you have become acquainted with the principal options of your iPad or iPhone with *iOS 10*. Of course, the iPad and iPhone contain many more interesting options. Take some time to browse through the many possible settings you can make in the individual apps and the *Settings* app and see if this can help to make your iPad or iPhone easier to use and even more to your liking.

5.9 Visual Steps Website and Newsletter

By now we hope you have noticed that the Visual Steps method is an excellent method for quickly and efficiently learning more about computers, tablets, other devices and software applications. All books published by Visual Steps use this same method.
In various series, we have published a large number of books on a wide variety of topics including *Windows*, *MacOS*, the iPad, iPhone, Samsung Galaxy Tab, photo editing and many other topics.

On the **www.visualsteps.com** website you will find a full product summary by clicking the blue *Catalog* button. For each book there is an extensive description, the full table of contents and a sample chapter (PDF file). In this way, you can quickly determine if a specific title will meet your expectations. You can order a book directly online from this website or other online book retailers. All titles are also available in bookstores in the USA, Canada, United Kingdom, Australia and New Zealand.

Furthermore, the website offers many extras, among other things:
- free computer guides and booklets (PDF files) covering all sorts of subjects;
- frequently asked questions and their answers;
- information on the free Computer Certificate that you can acquire at the certificate's website **www.ccforseniors.com**;
- a free email notification service: let's you know when a new book is published.

There is always more to learn. Visual Steps offers many other books on computer-related subjects. Each Visual Steps book has been written using the same step-by-step method with short, concise instructions and screenshots illustrating every step.

Would you like to be informed when a new Visual Steps title becomes available? Subscribe to the free Visual Steps newsletter (no strings attached) and you will receive this information in your inbox.
The Newsletter is sent approximately each month and includes information about
- the latest titles;
- supplemental information concerning titles previously released;
- new free computer booklets and guides;

When you subscribe to our Newsletter you will have direct access to the free booklets on the **www.visualsteps.com/info_downloads.php** web page.

5.10 Tips

 Tip

Updating or resetting your choice

If you are not satisfied with the suggestions you get from *Apple Music* based on your choice of genres and artists, you can adjust your choice as follows:

To start all over again:

☞ **Tap** Reset

☞ **Follow the steps you have done earlier in this chapter**

You can also delete genres or artists, or give them less preference, in the choices you already made. Adding already deleted genres or artists is not possible.

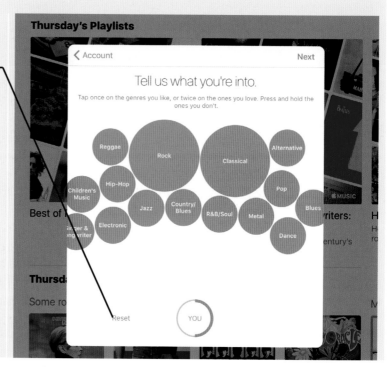

 Tip

AirPods

With the introduction of *iOS 10,* Apple introduced a new type of wireless earplugs as well. These AirPods do not have wires anymore, and if you put them in your ears, they are immediately connected to your iPad or iPhone. If you take them out again, the music pauses.

You can also use *Siri* by tapping twice on one of the AirPods. It lets you do things on your iPad or iPhone hands free.

Appendix A. Glossary

Account	A combination of a username and password for gaining access to a protected service.
AirPods	Apple's wireless earbud type of headphone.
App	Abbreviation of *application*, a program for the iPad or iPhone.
App Store	Apple's online store where you can download free or paid apps.
Apple ID	Combination of an email address and password, also called *iTunes App Store Account*. You need an *Apple ID* for, among others, downloading apps from the *App Store*.
Apple Music	Apple's streaming music service that lets you listen to unlimited music for a fixed monthly fee (first three month trial is free).
Auto-Lock	Standard feature that ensures that the iPad or iPhone, when it is not used, is locked after a set time.
Badge	A symbol displayed on an app, such as ▆. This is an indication of a warning, the number of new messages or other notifications.
Bluetooth	Open standard for wireless connections between devices at close range. You can use Bluetooth to connect a wireless keyboard, AirPods or headset to the iPad or iPhone.
Bookmark	Reference to a web address, saved in a list. You can access a web page much faster by creating a bookmark for it.
Calendar	App for keeping track of your activities and appointments.
Camera	App that lets you take pictures and videos. You can either use the camera on the front or the one on the back of the iPad or iPhone.
Contacts	You can add and manage your contacts with this app.
Digital zoom	In a digital zoom just a small part from the original image is enlarged. You see no extra details, only the pixels are enlarged and the quality however is reduced.

FaceTime	App that lets you make free video calls through the Internet with contacts around the world. The disadvantage of *FaceTime* is that it only allows contact with other iPad, iPhone or Mac users.
Favorites	Favorite websites, stored in a list.
Gmail	*Google*'s free web-based email service.
Home button	The button ⬭ that lets you return to the home screen. With this button you can wake up the iPhone and iPad from sleep mode.
Home screen	The first screen with app icons you see when you open or unlock the iPad or iPhone.
iBooks	App that lets you read eBooks (electronic books) and PDF files. PDF files are often easier to read in *iBooks* rather than *Safari*, for example.
iCloud	Apple's cloud storage service. It gives you access to your documents and data from a variety of devices.
iCloud Drive	You can think of *iCloud Drive* as a kind of online USB stick. *iCloud Drive* lets you store all kinds of files, even if they are not designed for Apple software. These files are synchronized to all devices where you have activated *iCloud Drive*. On devices where *iCloud Drive* is not activated, you can look at and manage the files through the *iCloud* website.
IMAP	IMAP stands for *Internet Message Access Protocol*. This means that you manage your email messages on the mail server. Messages that are already read remain on the server until you delete them. IMAP is useful if you manage your email from multiple devices. Your mailbox will then look the same on every computer, tablet or phone. When you create folders to organize your email, the same folders will usually appear on the other computers, and on your iPad or iPhone as well. To use IMAP, you need to set up your email account as IMAP.
iMessage	Feature that lets you send free messages to other iPhone, iPad and iPod Touch users over 3G, 4G or Wi-Fi. When sent over 3G or 4G, data charges may be incurred, but a text message is usually a small file and often no more than 140 bytes.
Inbox	Folder in *Mail* where you can view your received email messages.

iOS	Mobile operating system developed by Apple for the iPad, iPhone, iPod Touch and Apple TV.
iTunes	Program that helps you manage your iPhone's contents. Furthermore, you can use *iTunes* to listen to music, watch video files and import CDs. In *iTunes*, you will also find the *iTunes* Store and *App Store*.
iTunes Library	List of songs stored in *iTunes* on your computer.
Library	The section of *iTunes* where you store and manage your music, movies, books, podcasts, apps and more.
Location Services	*Location Services* allows apps, such as *Maps*, to collect and use information about your location. The collected information is not tied to your personal information. If you are connected to the Internet and have turned on *Location Services*, information about the location will be added, for example, to the photos and videos you make with your iPad or iPhone.
Mail	Default app on the iPad or iPhone allowing you to send and receive email messages.
Maps	App that helps you search for locations and addresses, look at satellite photos and plan routes.
Messages	App that lets you send an SMS or (if necessary) an *iMessage*.
Music	App that lets you play music.
Notes	App for jotting down notes.
Notification Center	Central feature for displaying messages, alerts, news flashes and more that you receive on your iPad or iPhone. You can decide what notifications are allowed to appear in the *Notification Center*. You open this feature by dragging down from the top of your screen.
Outlook.com	*Microsoft's* free web-based email service.
Photos	App for viewing the photos and videos on your iPad or iPhone.
Playlist	A collection of songs in a certain order. You can use a playlist, for example, to play your favorite music.

POP POP stands for *Post Office Protocol*, the traditional way to manage email. When you retrieve your email, messages are immediately deleted from the server. However, the POP accounts on your iPhone or iPad are set by default to keep a copy on the server. This way you can retrieve your email on your computer as well.

Reminders In the *Reminders* app you can store important appointments or tasks and set a date or time to be alerted.

Ringtone Melody or sound you hear when you receive a call.

Safari Apple's web browsing app.

Search my iPad/iPhone Option for locating your iPad or iPhone on a map. By logging in via a web browser on the *iCloud* website, you can let your iPad or iPhone be displayed on a map. In addition, you can remotely lock your iPad or iPhone and let it show a message to anyone who finds your device.

Siri Feature that allows you to give instructions to the iPad or iPhone by spoken text.

Sleep mode When you are not using it, you can lock the iPhone by switching to sleep mode. If the iPad or iPhone is locked, nothing happens when you would touch the screen. However, you are still reachable for phone calls and music or podcasts will continue to play. You can also adjust the volume. You can use the sleep/wake button on the upper or right side of your device to turn on sleep mode.

Slide Over Opens a second app in a narrow panel on the right-hand side of the screen.

SMS Stands for *short message service*, a service that lets you send short text messages and receive data over a mobile network. Your mobile provider will usually charge a fixed rate per sent text message. Receiving an SMS is free.

Split View Feature that allows you to use two apps simultaneously.

Spotlight The search function on the iPad and iPhone.

Streaming Method for transferring data (music, podcasts, video and more) over the Internet in a continuous stream to your device. You are not downloading any files.

Trash

Mail folder in which your deleted messages are saved. Once you delete a message from the *Trash*, it is permanently deleted.

WhatsApp

Messaging service app similar to *iMessage*. *WhatsApp* can be used on the iPhone and other smartphones. It can be downloaded from the *App Store*.

Source: User Manual iPad and iPhone, Wikipedia

Appendix B. Index

Photo Editing on the iPad for SENIORS

There is so much you can do with an iPad. But one of the best applications is surely working with photos! There are many apps available that come with a variety of tools for enhancing your photos. You can spruce up the photos you took from a memorable event or vacation for example, and share them with others. And what about making a collage, slideshow or photo album?

> *HAVE FUN AND BECOME A PHOTO EDITING EXPERT ON YOUR IPAD!*

This user-friendly book shows you in a jiffy how to create and edit all of these types of projects. A number of photo editing apps are easy to use and free to download. They offer lots of preset filters, plus useful tools to crop, repair, lighten, darken or sharpen your photos. And if you want additional editing capability, you can purchase an app for a small amount with even more great features. You will learn how to use these apps with clear step-by-step instructions. You can get started right away with exercise pictures that can be downloaded from our website.

With the knowledge and experience you gain, you will soon be able to edit your own photos and turn them into works of art. It will surprise you how much is possible with photos on the iPad!

Author: Studio Visual Steps
ISBN 978 90 5905 731 9
Book type: Paperback, full color
Nr of pages: 312
Accompanying website:
www.visualsteps.com/photoipad

Full color!

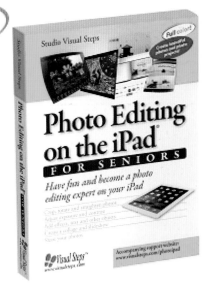

Learn how to:
- Crop, rotate and straighten photos
- Adjust exposure and contrast
- Add effects, text and other objects
- Create a collage and slideshow
- Share your photos

Suitable for: all iPads.

Windows 10 for SENIORS

> **GET STARTED QUICKLY WITH WINDOWS 10**

Windows 10 for Seniors is the ideal book for seniors who have worked with an earlier version of Windows on a desktop or laptop computer and want to get started right away with Windows 10. All of the most important topics are covered, such as using the Internet safely, sending and receiving email and working with files and folders. You will also learn how to organize and view photos and videos and listen to music in Windows 10.

Step by step, in your own tempo, you will get acquainted with the new and renewed programs in Windows 10. You will get familiar with the new Start menu and learn how to adjust the settings to make Windows 10 easier and more comfortable to work with. The book contains additional exercises to repeat and reinforce everything you have learned. Instructional videos are also available on the website that accompanies this book. They explain how to perform specific tasks.

In no time at all you will become comfortable and at ease with Windows 10!

Author: Studio Visual Steps
ISBN 978 90 5905 451 6
Book type: Paperback, full color
Nr of pages: 320 pages
Accompanying website:
www.visualsteps.com/windows10

Full color!

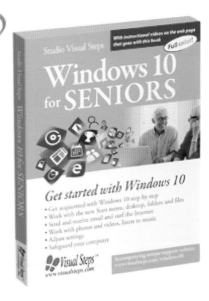

Learn how to:
- Get acquainted with Windows 10 step-by-step
- Work with the new Start menu, desktop, folders and files
- Send and receive email and surf the Internet
- Work with photos and videos, listen to music
- Adjust settings
- Safeguard your computer

Suitable for:
Windows 10 on a desktop or laptop computer